Decks and Patios

Designing and Building Outdoor Living Spaces

Decks and Patios

Designing and Building Outdoor Living Spaces

Edward A. Baldwin

TAB BOOKS
Blue Ridge Summit, PA

FIRST EDITION
SECOND PRINTING

© 1990 by **Edward A. Baldwin**
Published by TAB BOOKS.
TAB BOOKS is a division of McGraw-Hill, Inc.

Library of Congress Cataloging-in-Publication Data

Baldwin, Edward A.
    Decks and patios : designing and building outdoor living spaces /
by Edward A. Baldwin.
     p.   cm.
    ISBN 0-8306-8326-7   ISBN 0-8306-3326-X (pbk.)
    1. Decks (Architecture, Domestic)—Design and construction.
2. Patios—Design and construction. I. Title.
TH4970.B35 1990
690.89—dc20   89-20601
                                                    CIP

TAB BOOKS offers software for sale. For information and a catalog, please contact
TAB Software Department, Blue Ridge Summit, PA 17294-0850.

Questions regarding the content of this book should be addressed to:

Reader Inquiry Branch
TAB BOOKS
Blue Ridge Summit, PA 17294-0850

Acquisitions Editor: Kimberly Tabor
Book Editor: Susan L. Rockwell
Production: Katherine G. Brown

This book is dedicated with great appreciation to Paul and Shirley Fischer who patiently put up with the mess and the delay so we finally got a great deck project built. Especially to Paul, who did all the work.

Contents

Acknowledgments

Author: Ed Baldwin
Editor and technical consultant: Peter Lippincott
Photography: Intermatic Inc., Hickson Corp., and Ed Baldwin
Art and Graphics: A World of Graphics, Inc.
Deck Construction: Klaus Lambert, Lambert Home Improvements
Project Designs: Ed Baldwin
Deck Materials: Hickson Corp., "Wolmanized Extra"™
Deck Lighting: Intermatic Inc.
Deck Connectors: Simpson Strong-Tie® Co. Inc.

A special thanks to Charlie and Barb Gillick, David and Janet Hoven, Steve and Sugar Rufer and other residents of Lake-Wood Hills who graciously allowed us to photograph their patio and deck projects for inclusion in this book. A very special thanks to Steve Rufer who patiently steadied the ladder while we photographed his lovely trilevel patio. The hand-held power tools we used were provided by RYOBI. The deck banisters and railings were ripped to shape using a Shopsmith Mark V.

Introduction

In writing this book, my first thoughts were to keep it as basic, simple, and straightforward as possible. There is no real magic in putting up a deck or laying a patio. There are some basic guidelines to make certain the deck will stay in place or that the patio will not crack. There are certain materials that work better than others. There are some construction guidelines that can make the difference between a well-constructed or poorly constructed project. I hope that I have adequately covered those points and have given you the information you need to complete the project of your choice properly. The materials I have suggested you use are designed to last as long as possible to avoid having to rebuild. There are certain ravages of nature that will undo even the best of projects if not properly protected. Please do remember that the project will need care over the years to ensure a long life. My family and I hope you have fun; good luck with your project and thank you for buying this book.

1

The Design Criteria
for Patios and Decks

DECKS AND PATIOS ARE NORMALLY DESIGNED TO PROVIDE AN OUTDOOR ENTERTAINMENT OR EX-
terior living area for your home. They can complement the architecture of your house,
add a new living dimension to your property, increase the value of your home, and impress
your neighbors. This book has been written to provide you a balanced look at both the
design and construction techniques for building patios and decks. It has been written to
give you the basic background information necessary to complete your own deck or patio
project with confidence and hopefully, to do it right.

THE PURPOSES DECKS AND PATIOS SERVE

The reasons for building a deck or patio can be as simple as trying to cover up the backyard so you have less grass to cut. Or, it might be that you have some sort of problem to deal
with and a patio or deck will provide the solution to the problem. There are numerous reasons to design a patio or deck.

1. Cover difficult terrain.

2. Satisfy your need for privacy.

3. Provide shade or shelter.

4. Cover unsightly yard conditions.

5. Satisfy your desire for an exterior living area.

6. Provide access to an upper level of your house.

7. Extend the space in your house for parties or entertainment.

The list can go on and on, but if you're reading this book, chances are you have a problem to solve. A properly designed deck or patio might be the solution.

The lay of your land will affect the design for a deck or patio. Steeply sloping hillsides
and gently rolling terrain provide both challenges and opportunities for unique and pleasant designs (Fig. 1-1).

Large expanses of grass yard can be broken up with both patio and deck designs. By
integrating both, you can create a garden living area that combines natural materials with
plants and flowers as well.

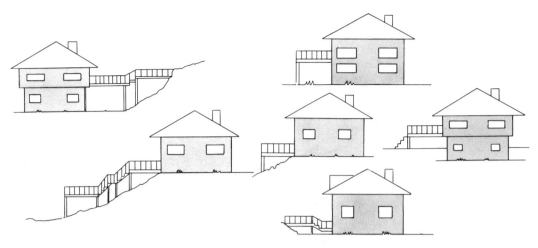

Fig. 1-1. A deck can be adapted to almost any terrain or integrated into your living scheme to take advantage of the unique construction of your home.

Unless your home is in a secluded area where privacy is not important, privacy screening can add a measure of seclusion. When integrated with your deck or patio a well-designed screening system can add considerable beauty to your home and create exterior comfort zones that will add to the value of your property.

In our urban and suburban environment today where trees are removed to build houses, some form of shade can add immeasurably to your backyard comfort. We will show you some successful shading techniques that look handsome too.

Do you have an unsightly rock pile? A place where grass won't grow? Do you have an old cracked slab of concrete you want to hide? A new deck or patio might be the solution you have hoped for.

Quite often the floor level of your house is more than a step above ground. A deck with steps makes a perfect transition from the ground level to your doorstep (Fig. 1-2).

Today's decks and patios are the modern version of the old-fashioned backporch. With the availability of modern materials and techniques the options for appearance, size, and function are enormous.

THE FUNCTIONAL VERSUS ESTHETIC DESIGN CONSIDERATIONS

No deck or patio design will be entirely functional. None of these projects are likely to be built solely for beauty. Each project will fall somewhere on the function/beauty continuum.

Perhaps all you need is a slab of concrete to provide a sitting area outside where your son can also ride his skateboard. Or, maybe you only need a straight shot of steps from the ground to your entry way. The size of your pocketbook might be the determining factor in the final design you select. But take a moment to think. There are inexpensive options that add greatly to the final appearance of your project. They also add value to your home when you get ready to sell.

By integrating concrete, found rocks and stone, and a few old railroad ties you can create a garden patio. By making stone planting beds and using the railroad ties to make raised planting borders your patio becomes very interesting, beautiful, and functional as well. The difference between a ho-hum slab of concrete and a great patio is minimal.

By creating a multilevel deck with shading and screening, you can create privacy areas that are great for intimacy at parties. This serves both function and beauty. By substituting inexpensive lattice for solid wood partitions, you save money. By combining materials properly, you can get the appearance of a very expensive deck for a lot less.

By using treated lumber for the deck foundation and redwood for the trim, floor, and rails, you get a redwood deck for a lot less. Through the use of proper stains and sealers, you can turn inexpensive lumber into very attractive decking.

Modified 12-volt lighting systems are simple to install and cheap. They give plenty of light for your evening parties and when the party is over, they add an element of security to your home.

You are only limited by your imagination when it comes to design. By carefully looking at all your options, the difference between a great project and one that is not so great might only be pennies.

PATIOS VERSUS DECKS

It might be helpful to explain the difference between a deck and a patio. Any structure that is built on the ground is a patio. An example of this would be a slab of concrete, bricks, or wooden pallets that lie directly on the ground. A deck, by contrast, is a wooden structure that is supported by a system of joists on a foundation. The distance above the ground is not important (see Fig. 1-2).

There are advantages and disadvantages to both decks and patios. Neither choice can always be the best solution to all landscaping, access, or living area problems. You must consider your desires and the problems you need to solve when choosing to build a deck, a patio, or a combination of the two.

The main advantage of a deck is that it can be built at any height above ground. This flexibility makes it possible to match an outdoor living space to any door level or access area of the house. Decks and steps can be used to bridge between different levels of your home such as between a first floor and a walk-out basement level (Fig. 1-3).

When the structure you need must be on the ground, or close to the ground, a patio is

Fig. 1-2. This is an excellent example of a ground-level deck.

Fig. 1-3. This is one example of unique approaches to building a deck to expand the livability of your home.

the best choice. The selection of materials is much larger for a patio than those for a deck. The construction cost is also normally much less. Patios can have a very long life when properly built from stone or stone like materials.

TYPES OF DECKS

Ground-level Decks

This is the most common form of deck. As the name *ground-level* would imply, these decks are built on the ground. In our discussion, however, we refer to ground-level decks as any structure on the ground up to a height of four to five feet. In fact unless a pit is dug to hold the joists and supporting foundation, the lowest deck would be approximately one foot off the ground. If the wood lies directly on the ground without a supporting foundation, it is a patio (Fig. 1-4).

High-rise Decks

High-rise decks are usually built in response to site conditions such as access to an upper-level doorway or the desire to catch a certain view of the surrounding area. These are superior structures when access to the sun and breeze are important. The height of this type of deck necessitates proper sizing of the supporting columns and bracing, which is an extremely important factor for stability (Fig. 1-5).

Multilevel Decks

A *multilevel* deck offers a unique response to the solution of many problems at once. It can allow for varied usage based on the criteria for sun/shade, privacy, and breeze. When used for a party, a multilevel deck will allow more intimate groupings of people to form. This type of deck is often very attractive and enhances the appearance of your home significantly (Fig. 1-6).

Load-bearing Decks

As the name implies, a *load-bearing* deck is one that must support an unusual weight. That is, more than the normal backyard variety deck. These structures are normally built to

Fig. 1-4. A ground-level deck is easy to build.

Fig. 1-5. High-rise decks give access to upper-level living areas and create enhanced value for your property. They also allow for separate living and entrance areas.

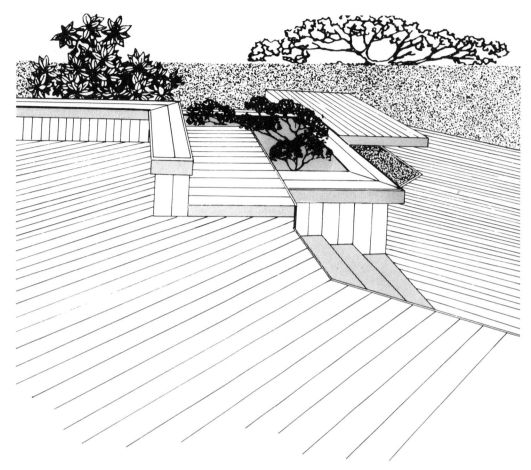

Fig. 1-6. A multilevel deck can level out the terrain in your backyard and turn an otherwise difficult terrain into an exceptional outdoor living area.

solve such problems as how to house a motor vehicle in a carport built over a hillside (Fig. 1-7). When the cost of excavation to level an area is prohibitive, this type of deck might be the only economical solution to the problem. The materials used in this deck and the supporting columns and foundations are substantially stronger than the average backyard deck. It is advisable to seek the advice of a professional if this is the kind of deck you need to construct.

Rooftop Decks

If your yard condition is crowded, a *rooftop* deck might be the one for you. Many houses are constructed with upper windows that could be converted into doors. Perhaps you have an attic that could be converted into a family room. A rooftop deck is a natural extension for this type of environment (Fig. 1-8).

This kind of deck takes advantage of the house's existing foundation. Stability concerns are usually not a major factor in building this deck.

Roofs can be either nearly flat or sloped. It is easier to construct a deck on a nearly level roof (Fig. 1-9). A sloped deck requires additional supports to achieve a level condition, whereas a nearly level roof deck can be leveled with simple blocking.

A prime concern in building a rooftop deck is avoiding damage to the roof and not impeding the run-off of water when it rains. For sloped roofs, your deck structure will make it impossible to replace the roof in years to come. It is advisable to replace the roof before adding the deck. Be certain that the supports or fasteners for your deck do not pierce nor wear away the roofing to cause leaks.

Fig. 1-7. Decks can be built to withstand very heavy loads and turn unusable space into functional units such as this carport.

Fig. 1-8. The roof of your house can be used to provide a deck with a scenic view of the neighborhood.

Fig. 1-9. This is a good example of expanding a second-floor room by converting the roof of one side of a house into a second-level deck.

TYPES OF PATIOS

Single-level or Ground-level Patios

All patios are built on the ground. Where the area to be used is fairly level and big enough, one single patio can be constructed. It is important that the surface be properly prepared and brought to a nearly level condition (Fig. 1-10). A slight pitch is always necessary to allow for the proper run-off of water and to avoid the collection of pools or pockets of water when it rains.

Fig. 1-10. This unique combination of wood, brick, and concrete combine to form steps to a ground-level patio.

Terraced and Multilevel Patios

Similar to multilevel decks, a *multilevel* patio can add a varied visual interest to your backyard (Fig. 1-11). Since few patio sites are totally level, it is easier to construct a patio that follows the natural lay of the land. By building walkways that slope or steps to each new level, you can create interesting multipatios that take advantage of an otherwise difficult piece of land (Fig. 1-12).

Terraced patios are multilevel patios made with a series of aligned steplike levels.

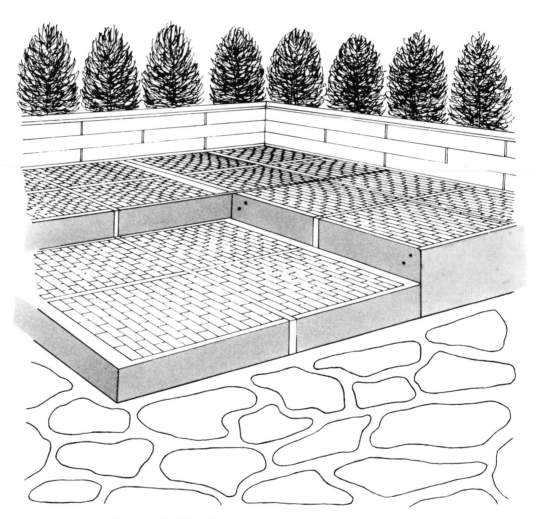

Fig. 1-11. Multilevel patios can take advantage of sloping ground.

Fig. 1-12. Decks and patios can be integrated as in this example to enclose an inground pool and spa that take advantage of the terrain slope.

Fig. 1-13. Railroad ties or timbers mixed with brick combine to create an interesting walkway and staircase.

Fig. 1-14. Patios and decks can be combined to create interesting private nooks and crannys.

WALKWAYS AND STAIRS

Walkways and steps can be made into interesting and unusual pathways around the outside of your house (Fig. 1-13). You can incorporate planting beds for flowers or low-voltage lighting to show the way at night. Plus, you can choose from a wide variety of materials. You can use broken or straight patterns to create the kinds of paths you want to the various parts of your yard, driveway, patio, or deck.

Walkways can be paved or made with loose material, stone, or wood products (Fig. 1-14). Some typical pavings include: concrete, either poured or in block form, bricks, stone, wooden blocks or logs, and asphalt. Loose material comes in the form of various sizes of gravel, small rocks, lava stone, sand, wood chips, and bark.

Steps can be made of similar materials including railroad ties. The details of construction are found later in this book.

2

Patio and Deck Design, Construction, and Layout Considerations

SIZE AND PLACEMENT CONSIDERATIONS

WHEN PLANNING A DECK OR PATIO IT IS IMPORTANT TO FIRST CONSIDER THE PRESENT USE OF your home's living area and yard space. How will your new project integrate with your existing property? Will the new project expand the present use? Will it complement or interfere with the existing area? What is the traffic flow? How many people must it serve? Who is going to use it? How big does it have to be? Is it going to pull routine traffic into an area of your house you don't want used on a regular basis? All of these things need to be considered.

The most common placement of decks and patios is off the family room or kitchen. In these cases the outdoor space is intended to be used by the entire family. Such functions as eating, sunning, game playing, lounging, and parties will be served through the passageway from the deck or patio into your house. How much traffic can that area handle? Installing a secondary access like a window with a shelf or bar through which you can pass food and drinks might be just the answer.

Normally, the placement of patios or decks is intended to expand the function of the room it is attached to. For example, placement off the dining area or living room would allow for fair weather dining or parties (Fig. 2-1). Perhaps the layout of your house and yard makes this placement necessary. If so, consider the traffic factor since the rug and nearby furniture will quickly show the results.

Less common, but a delightful idea, is a deck or patio off the master bath or bedroom, a normally very private space (Fig. 2-2). With proper screening, you can eliminate the need for curtains and obscure glass and bring the outdoors into your private world.

When determining the size of the patio or deck you wish to build there are certain immediate factors to consider. What is your budget? How many people must it serve? What limitations are there from local building codes? How much space is available? If you are building a rooftop deck, the size of the roof might be the limitation.

Deck or patio size can be directly related to the number of people it will serve. A good rule-of-thumb is 20 square feet per person for lounging, *suning*, and dining. Visualize an area 4 feet × 5 feet. In that area you have room for a chair, a small table, and some space to

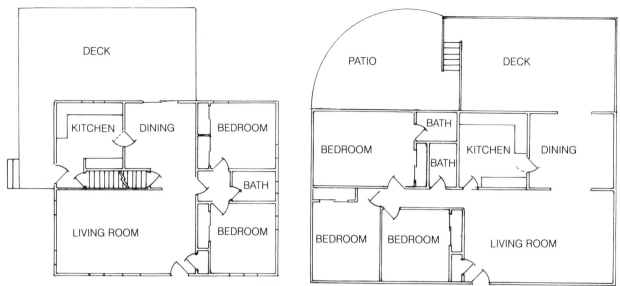

Fig. 2-1. Decks or patios should be built with the house traffic in mind.

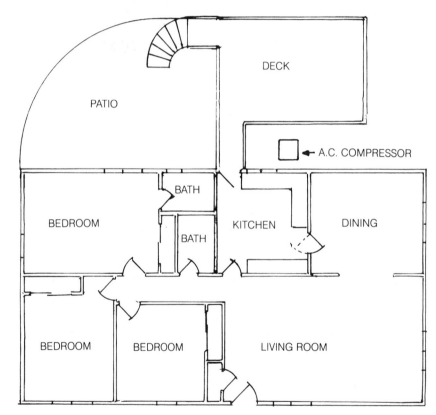

Fig. 2-2. A patio off of a bedroom can provide outdoor privacy.

move around. If you are planning to use an outdoor dining table, leave at least 30 inches on all sides for chairs and space to move in. For a 4-foot round table the minimal deck space would be 9 feet × 9 feet.

The above guidelines would translate into twenty people needing 400 square feet or a space 20 feet × 20 feet. Fifty people would need 1000 square feet or a space 25 feet × 40 feet. Obviously if you have a party where many people stand, more people could be accommodated in a pinch. Make certain the deck is built to hold the weight.

SELECTING THE SITE FOR CONSTRUCTION

In determining the site or location of your deck or patio, there are several factors that have to be considered: easements, utilities, electrical needs, soil conditions, terrain, and finally, the building or site that it must relate to.

You might have owned your home for a long time and are still not aware of any easements. A bad time to find out about easements is after the project is built. Will you be building over any utilitie's right-of-way? Water, telephones, gas, and electric are all installed underground in most home sites today. If you start digging footings, you don't want to have an electrifying experience or a temporary loss of phone service.

If you do not have a survey of your property, now might be a good time to obtain one (Fig. 2-3). This can usually be found at the county or city property tax office or the county courthouse. Your survey should show all easements and any restrictions associated with your property. It will not show entrance points and paths of underground services.

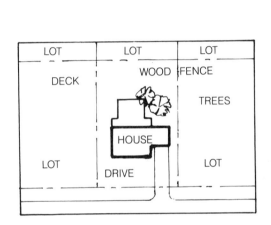

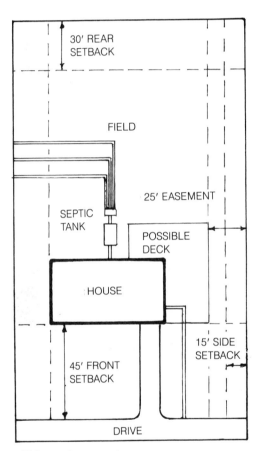

Fig. 2-3. Make certain you know where your utilities and easements are.

If you plan to install a gas grill or lighting you have to determine where the access point is for these utilities. Wiring or plumbing will have to be done after the excavation but before pouring the foundations or slabs. It is extremely important to install ground fault systems for exterior wiring. Consider the use of 12-volt lighting systems; they are safe and inexpensive.

The soil conditions are usually a minor consideration in the construction of a deck or patio, but the following detail should be noted. Soils with heavy clay content can swell and move after heavy rains. If you have clay soil the use of control joists in a concrete patio will minimize damage. Proper support for any foundation should be on virgin soil not fill dirt. Where permits and inspections are required, you are likely to be rejected unless the structure is on soil that is well compacted. Independent posts that support decks should rest on concrete piers in holes dug down into the virgin ground level. The use of concrete blocks or stones as piers resting on the surface soil is not recommended (Fig. 2-4). The depth required to avoid frost heaving problems varies with the severity of your winter.

Take a long hard look at your existing yard plantings, trees, shrubs, and the bricks or wood used in your house. How can you integrate your new deck or patio so that it complements your existing structure? Make certain that the deck wood matches the wood of your house or that the patio bricks integrate well with the bricks used in your house. Ask your local nursery men how you can build around existing shrubs and trees without disturbing them or causing damage. You might want to remove trees or shrubs with questionable life expectancy before you install the new project.

The final consideration is the terrain. The easiest situation to work with in building a deck or patio is a relatively level land that gently slopes away from your house. On the other hand, a challenging terrain can require a unique solution that can result in a very attractive project. Patios should be nearly level with about a 5 percent grade for drainage. Decks with spaced decking can be made level. Decks with tongue-and-groove decking that are solid must have a slight incline to shed water properly. Ground that slopes away from your house is ideal for decking since you can install steps of varying heights and lengths depending on the distance to the ground. Patios in this situation must be terraced.

Fig. 2-4. This slab was poured on fill dirt. The pier to the right saved the slab from slipping and cracking.

BUILDING CODES AND PERMITS

Building codes and permits are required in those municipalities that have passed laws governing the use of the land. These laws are generally passed in the interest of the homeowners to protect the property values of the neighborhood. They normally pertain to land use (zoning), setback requirements (how close to your property line you can build), and public safety.

Building a project without obtaining the appropriate permit can be very time consuming and expensive. Inspectors have the right to ask you to remove your structure, apply for a permit, and then rebuild. If that does not suffice, in many cases, they have the power to get a court order. If you refuse to obey a court order, the court can find you in contempt and put you in jail. All in all, it is much easier to get a permit in the first place and grit your teeth as you go through the inspection process.

It is advisable to find out what the inspector is going to be looking for. It can be frustrating to dig your foundation hole and then have to wait for an inspection. It can be more frustrating to be required to remove the concrete so the inspector can see the condition of the soil underneath. Inspectors are especially critical of the compliance with codes for exterior wiring and other utilities, that if improperly installed, could harm someone.

WEATHER AND CLIMATE CONSIDERATIONS

The weather in your area is a very important factor in your selection of materials from which to construct your deck and patio. Wind, rain, snow, ice, and the sun will all take their toll on your project once it is finished. Ideas for protecting your work and how to minimize damage is discussed in later chapters. The weather and the outdoor living conditions are equally important. In the Southwest, a wood patio might be the best way to stay cool, whereas in the Northeast, brick or asphalt is acceptable to retain the heat in the spring and fall months.

Track the sun's angle to your property over the winter and summer months. How can you take advantage of the sun's rays in the winter for warmth and yet reflect or block those same rays to keep your deck or patio cool in the summer months?

The sun will, in time, bleach the wood in your deck and patio project to a soft grey color. Moisture contributes to rotting the wood structures and causes the formation of slippery green moss to form on bricks. Sealing your deck with a proper exterior grade finish will deter the greying process and protect from the damaging effect of water. Sloping your deck or patio properly will ensure a proper run-off of water. Make certain your soil is properly prepared to resist erosion. Plantings, rocks, or terraces will help this.

Freezing water is one of nature's most destructive forces. The expansion that takes place when water freezes is enormous. It can crack concrete slabs, heave patios, lift footings out of the ground, crack bricks, and separate deck members. We will provide you with suggestions to protect your property against these problems in the construction section.

Wind is a factor to consider carefully. If your site has unusually strong wind, you might want to construct a wind break as part of your project design. Structurally, the patios and decks shown in this book can take a normal wind load. A lightly constructed roof with the wrong angle can act as a sail in the wind. Plastic or canvas roofing can be buffeted to the point of tearing and shredding if not properly fastened or installed to be easily removed.

Snow effects are similar to rain, but additionally involve snow load and freezing. Roofs, especially those above patios and decks, will freeze rapidly in the wind. They do not have the protection of slight warming from the house. Snow accumulation will add to the weight of the roof causing it to collapse. Proper construction will prevent this. If you live in an area of large snow falls, it would be wise to check with a local architect or engineer to get their advice. We will cover the basics in this book.

DECK MATERIALS AND HARDWARE

While concrete, brick, stone, asphalt, railroad ties, and wood could be the choices for patios, wood is the only reasonable choice for building decks. Commercial decks have been made from steel, plastic, and even concrete. For the average do-it-yourselfer, wood is the product of choice. The question, however, is which kind of wood?

Woods fall into two general categories, softwood and hardwood. Hardwoods such as oak, walnut, or maple are not normally used in deck construction. They do not have the natural resins necessary to protect them from decay, and they are too expensive. Of the softwoods that can be safely used outdoors, fir and cypress have a slight resistance to decay and rotting. However, the preferred wood for most outdoor projects is either redwood, western red cedar, or treated lumber.

Treated lumber is lumber soaked in a chromated copper arsenate solution in large sealed tanks. The solution is driven deep into the wood under pressure so that even when the board is cut the end cuts of the wood are protected (Fig. 2-5). This process is usually referred to as a Wolmanized treatment, which turns the wood a light green color. Yellow pine is usually the lumber so treated and when finished meets or exceeds the natural qualities to resist decay that are present in redwood and western red cedar. Yellow pine is also a much stronger wood. It should be noted here that only the heartwood of redwood and cedar are decay resistant.

A. BRUSHED-ON PRESERVATIVE

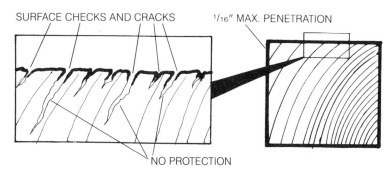

B. WOOD DIPPED OR SOAKED IN PRESERVATIVE

C. PRESSURE-TREATED

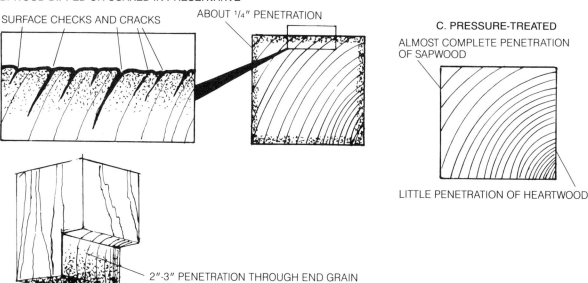

Fig. 2-5. A. BRUSHED-ON preservative rarely penetrates more than $^1/_{16}$ in. It also fails to completely coat exposed wood in cracks. B. DIPPING or soaking coats wood exterior thoroughly, up to about $^1/_4$-in. penetration on sides and 2 - 3 in. in end grain. Later, new cracks expose untreated wood, which is vulnerable to fungus. C. PRESSURE treatment penetrates about 85 percent of the sapwood, providing good protection. Heartwood is not penetrated and should be avoided when buying lumber.

In the past, paint-on wood treatments such as creosote or penta have been used to protect the wood members of decks and patios. These chemicals contain hazardous PCBs, which are dangerous and have been banned by the Environmental Protection Agency.

The costs of wood will vary depending on the grade, proximity to the source, and pricing policies of your local material yard. You will have to compare the relative merits versus the costs in making your selection of wood species.

Western red cedar is easy to work, smells good, and has a pleasant golden-red color. Because it is only moderately resistant to decay and insects, it is best used in areas that get enough sun to dry it after a rain. In some areas clear cedar (no knots) is only available on special order. Number 2 cedar, the most commonly available cedar, has knots that become loose and fall out in time. Cedar weathers to a light grey.

Redwood is about as soft as red cedar. It is also easy to work, smells good, and has a deep red color. Avoid the use of redwood sapwood, it is white and does not contain the protecting resins the heartwood contains. Redwood is very durable under damp conditions. It is available in both clear and construction grades. Obviously clear costs more money, but the difference in appearance is striking. You might want to pay more for wood used in exposed areas such as railings and decking. Redwood weathers to a variable grey, a light grey in sunny areas to almost black in damp shaded areas.

Pressure-treated yellow pine is considerably harder than redwood or cedar. It is more prone to splitting when nailed and has a strong tendency to twist and bow. Check the lumber when you buy it. Don't settle for twisted or bowed lumber at the materials yard. When you get your lumber to the construction site, stack it carefully so the weight will keep all the boards straight. Pressure-treated lumber also weathers to a light grey in time.

All of the aforementioned wood products are subject to destruction over a period of time by water and sun if they are not properly sealed and protected. Water, the primary culprit in the destruction of exterior wood projects, soaks into the wood, freezes, contracts, expands, and evaporates. The wood, over a period of time, is cracked, warped, split, checked, splintered, twisted, grain-raised, and destroyed. I have a western red cedar deck that is only nine years old, and yet many of the deckboards have deteriorated and need to be replaced (Fig. 2-6). The deck was painted with an exterior acrylic latex paint but was never properly sealed. Nine years is not very long; a deck should last a lifetime or longer.

Fig. 2-6. This is a plank of western cedar that was not treated properly. This deck is less than 8 years old and now needs replacement. Pressure-treated lumber should have been used.

A new category of pressure-treated lumber that resists water penetration has been introduced by the lumber industry as of this writing. We built the deck shown in this book using this new product. This product has all of the characteristics of regular pressure-treated lumber but has also been impregnated and pressure-treated with a chemical to shed water (Fig. 2-7). This product resists rot and insect infestation, and since it is pressure-treated to resist water, it has a better protection against water than you could obtain from sealants applied in the conventional manner. Even this product, however, requires the application of additional sealants to maximize the protection to the wood finish. In my opinion if you are going to use pressure-treated lumber for exterior work, this is the product of choice.

Fig. 2-7. Make certain that the lumber you are buying is properly marked.

Hardware is used to hold the wooden members of a deck together. It is usually metal and takes the form of nails, screws, bolts, plates, and various anchors (Fig. 2-8). Many municipalities now require the use of joist hangers, nailing plates, and hurricane ties. The most frequently used metal is galvanized steel; however, brass, aluminum, and stainless steel are also used.

Nails come in various forms, such as common, finish, casing, and deformed. Deformed nails have the superior and longer holding power. Treated nails are preferred; untreated nails will rust and stain the deck over a period of time.

Screws are the fastener of choice when putting decks together (Fig. 2-9). The common forms of screws are round head, oval head, and flat head. In most cases the flat head does the best job as it will draw down flush and not protrude above the surface. A new generation of galvanized flat head screws with a slotted Phillips head is available. It has a self-tapping action that minimizes splitting and automatically cuts a recess for the head. The better screw is one with a polymer and zinc coating called *Dacrotized* weather proofing. This product, a preboring fastener, is heat-treated and case-hardened.

Lag screws, another form of screw, are commonly used when fastening thick members, such as a 2 × 4 to an even thicker member such as a 4 × 4. A pilot hole must be drilled in

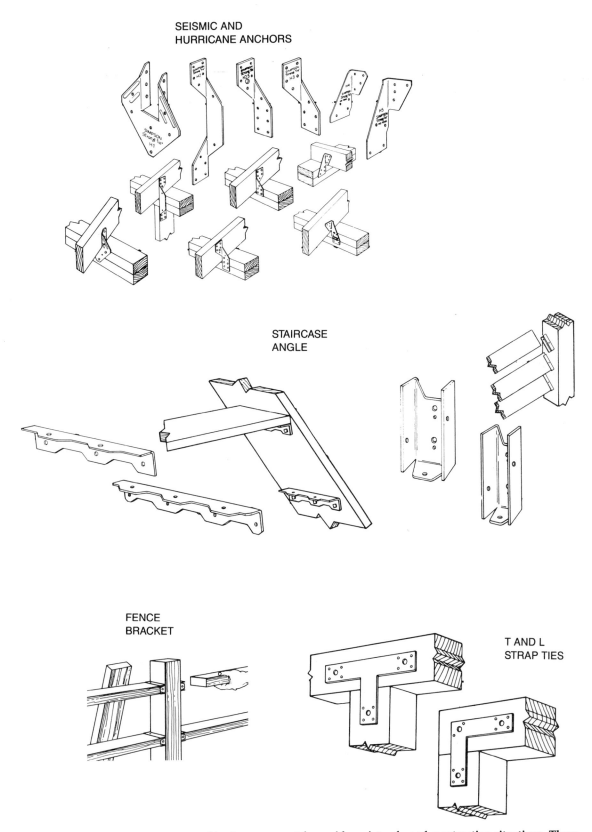

SEISMIC AND
HURRICANE ANCHORS

STAIRCASE
ANGLE

FENCE
BRACKET

T AND L
STRAP TIES

Fig. 2-8. Metal connectors provide strong support for a wide variety of wood construction situations. These products manufactured by the Simpson Strong-Tie Company are some examples of the many products that make deck construction easy.

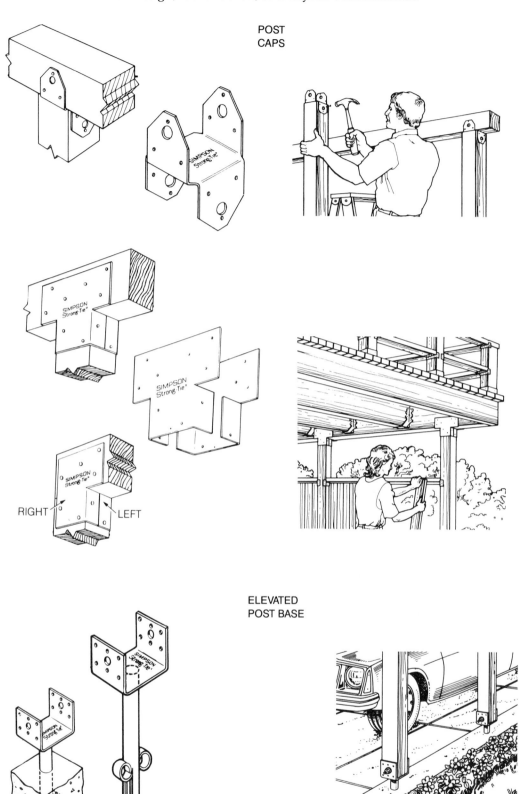

POST
CAPS

ELEVATED
POST BASE

Fig. 2-8. Continued.

POST BASES

ADJUSTABLE
POST BASE

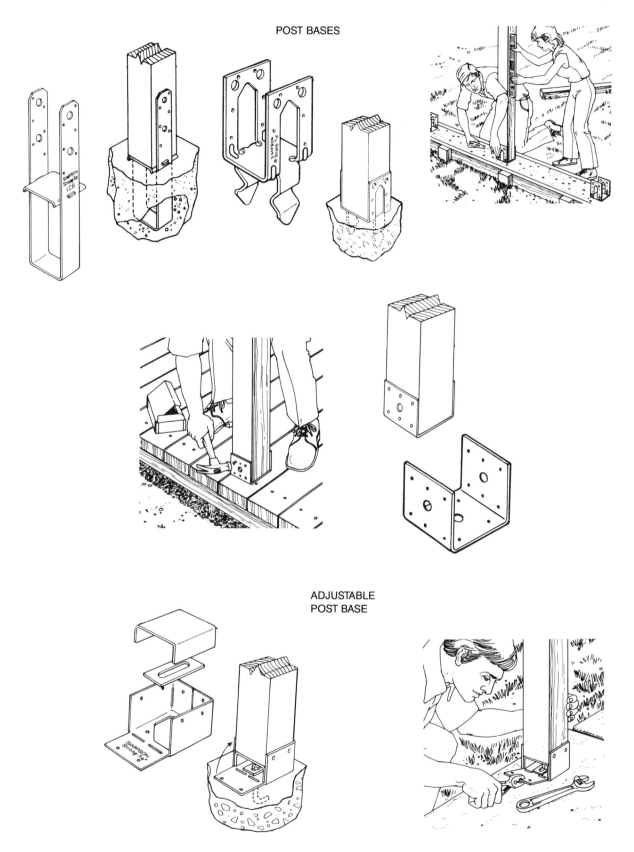

Fig. 2-8. Continued.

COLUMN
BASES

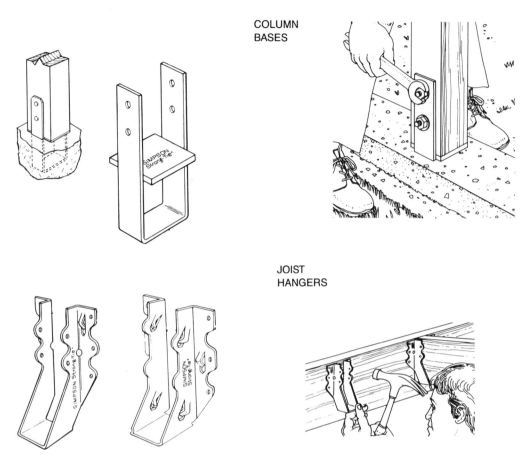

JOIST
HANGERS

Speed prongs position the hanger for header nailing and eliminate joist nailing and the use of special short nails.

SLANT NAILING

RIDGE RAFTER
CONNECTOR

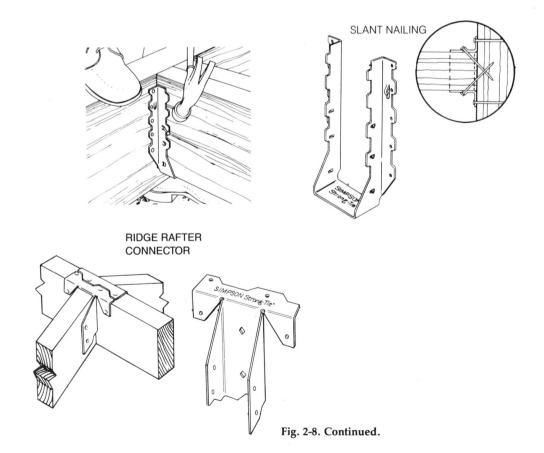

Fig. 2-8. Continued.

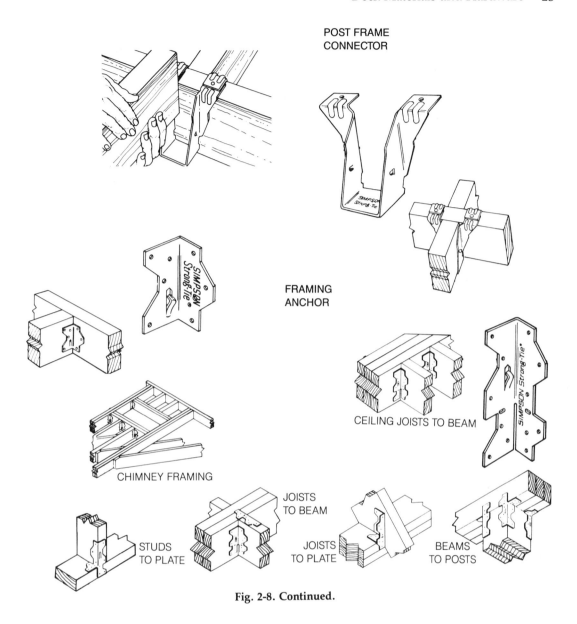

POST FRAME
CONNECTOR

FRAMING
ANCHOR

CEILING JOISTS TO BEAM

CHIMNEY FRAMING

STUDS
TO PLATE

JOISTS
TO BEAM

JOISTS
TO PLATE

BEAMS
TO POSTS

Fig. 2-8. Continued.

SELF DRILLING, SELF COUNTERSINKING SCREWS

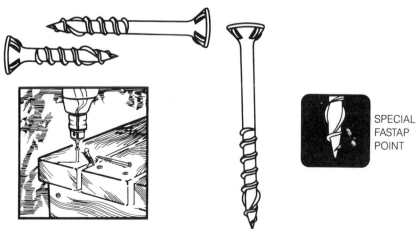

SPECIAL
FASTAP
POINT

Fig. 2-9. Make certain that the screws and nails you use for deck construction are rustproof.

the thinner wood member the size of the lag screw, $^2/_3$ to $^3/_4$ the diameter in the thicker member. A large washer should always be used under the head of a lag screw (Fig. 2-10).

Carriage bolts, another form of fastener, have a square shank under a domed head. This square shank bites into the wood and prevents the bolt from turning. Use a washer under the nut of a carriage bolt.

Machine bolts require a washer at both ends and are the preferred fastener for attaching large deck support boards together.

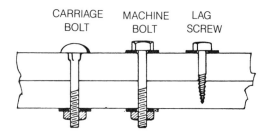

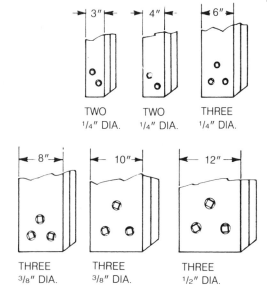

Fig. 2-10. The numbers and sizes of bolts or lag screws are dependent on the size and width of the lumber you are using.

CALCULATING POST, BEAM, AND JOIST SIZING FROM CHARTS

It is critical that a deck be built strong enough to withstand all of the normal pressure it will receive. These pressures come from the *dead weight* of the deck itself, the *live load*, furniture placed upon it, the people who walk on it, and the forces of nature such as wind, rain, and snow. We are basing our figures in these tables on a dead load weight of 10 pounds per square foot and a live load of 40 pounds per square foot. Even with this safety factor, any unusual weight such as a spa or a child's swimming pool should receive support from additional posts and beams directly under the object. Verify your special requirements with an engineer for safety.

Tables 2-1 through 2-5 contain the necessary information to build a sturdy deck. Please

Table 2-1. Joist Span Table

Joist	Max. span allowed when laid on edge	
2×6 (minimum)	@ 12 in. o.c.	8 ft.
	@ 16 in. o.c.	7 ft.
	@ 24 in. o.c.	5 ft.
2×8	@ 12 in. o.c.	10 ft.
	@ 16 in. o.c.	9 ft.
	@ 24 in. o.c.	7 ft.
2×10	@ 12 in. o.c.	13 ft.
	@ 16 in. o.c.	12 ft.
	@ 24 in. o.c.	10 ft.
2×12	@ 12 in. o.c.	16 ft.
	@ 16 in. o.c.	15 ft.
	@ 24 in. o.c.	14 ft.

O.C. stands for on center (of Joist)

Table 2-2. Minimum Beam Sizes and Spans

Species Group A Beam Size	4	5	6	7	8	9	10	11	12
4×6″ ×	6	6	6						
3×8″ ×	8	8	7	6	6	6			
4×8″ ×	10	9	8	7	7	6	6	6	
3×10″ ×	11	10	9	8	8	7	7	6	6
4×10″ ×	12	11	10	9	9	8	8	7	7
3×12″ ×		12	11	10	9	9	8	8	8
4×12″ ×			12	12	11	10	10	9	9
6×10″ ×					12	11	10	10	10
6×12″ ×						12	12	12	12
Species Group B									
4×6″ ×	6	6							
3×8″ ×	7	7	6	6					
4×8″ ×	9	8	7	7	6	6			
3×10″ ×	10	9	8	7	7	6	6	6	
4×10″ ×	11	10	9	8	8	7	7	7	6
3×12″ ×	12	11	10	9	8	8	7	7	7
4×12″ ×		12	11	10	10	9	9	8	8
6×10″ ×			12	11	10	10	9	9	9
6×12″ ×				12	12	12	11	11	10
Species Group C									
4×6″ ×	6								
3×8″ ×	7	6							
4×8″ ×	8	7	6	6					
3×10″ ×	9	8	7	6	6	6			
4×10″ ×	10	9	8	8	7	7	6	6	6
3×12″ ×	11	10	9	8	7	7	7	6	6
4×12″ ×	12	11	10	9	9	8	8	7	7
6×10″ ×		12	11	10	9	9	8	8	8
6×12″ ×			12	12	11	11	10	10	8

Beams are on edge. Spans are center to center distances between posts or supports. Grade is No. 2 or Better; No. 2, medium grain southern pine.

Species Group A. Douglas fir, larch, southern pine. *Species Group B.* Hemlock fir, Douglas fir, south. *Species Group C.* Western pines and cedars, redwood, spruces.

Example: If the beams are 9 ft. 8 in. apart and the species is Group B, use the 10 ft. column; 3×10 up to 6 ft. spans, 4×10 or 3×12 up to 7 ft. spans, 4×12 or 6×10 up to 9 ft. spans, 6×12 up to 11 ft. spans.

Table 2-3. Minimum Post Sizes (Wood Beam Supports)

Species Group A Post Size	Load Area Beam Spacing × Post Spacing, Sq. Ft.									
	36	48	60	72	84	96	108	120	132	144
4×4″ ×	12	12	12	12	10	10	10	8	8	8
4×6″ ×					12	12	12	12	10	10
6×6″ ×									12	12
Species Group B										
4×4″ ×	12	12	10	10	10	8	8	8	8	
4×6″ ×		12	12	12	10	10	10	10		
6×6″ ×					12	12	12	12	12	
Species Group C										
4×4″ ×	12	10	10	8	8	8	6	6	6	6
4×6″ ×		12	12	10	10	10	8	8	8	8
6×6″ ×				12	12	12	12	12	12	12

Grade is Standard and Better for 4×4 in. posts and No. 1 and Better for larger sizes.
Species Group A: Douglas fir, larch, southern pine. *Species Group B:* Hemlock fir, Douglas fir, southern fir. *Species Group C:* Western pines, western cedars, redwood, spruce.
Example: If the beams are spaced 8 ft. 6 in. on center and the posts are 11 ft. 6 in. on center, then the load area is 98 sq. ft. Use the next largest area, 108 sq. ft.

Table 2-4. Lumber Sizes

Nominal Size	Actual Size
1×2	3/4 × 1 1/2
1×3	3/4 × 2 1/2
1×4	3/4 × 3 1/2
1×6	3/4 × 5 1/2
1×8	3/4 × 7 1/4
1×10	3/4 × 9 1/4
1×12	3/4 × 11 1/4
2×2	1 1/2 × 1 1/2
2×3	1 1/2 × 2 1/2
2×4	1 1/2 × 3 1/2
2×6	1 1/2 × 5 1/2
2×8	1 1/2 × 7 1/4
2×10	1 1/2 × 9 1/4
2×12	1 1/2 × 11 1/4
4×4	3 1/2 × 3 1/2
6×6	5 1/2 × 5 1/2

Table 2-5. Beam Span Table

Beam Size	Max. Span Allowed When Laid on Edge
4×4 or two 2×4s	4 ft.
4×6 or two 2×6s	6 ft.
4×8 or two 2×8s	8 ft.
4×10 or two 2×10s	10 ft.
4×12 or two 6×10s	12 ft.
6×10 or three 2×10s	12 ft.
6×12 or three 2×12s	14 ft.

note there are two categories of wood strength in these tables. Pressure-treated pine is stronger than cedar or redwood.

The top structural layer, the decking, is not included the tables because the decking we have recommended (2 × 4, 2 × 6, and biased radius decking) will safely span the 16- or 24-inch joist spacing.

The next layer, the joists, can be calculated on their simple span between supports. A *support* means the wall of the house, a retaining wall, or a beam. Read the maximum span from Table 2-1.

The beams are next. Table 2-2 considers beams made from two or three boards. A beam made from three 2 × 8s will clearly carry more load than two 2 × 8s. To use the table read beam size on the left, distance between beams at the top, and spacing between posts from the field of the table.

Let's assume you want to build a 10-×-20-foot deck, which has the 20-foot side attached to the house. The outboard side (away from the house) must be supported with a beam. You have a given beam spacing of 10 feet from the house to the beam. Reading down the 10 foot column you can see that if you install a post every 6 feet, you can use a triple 2 × 8; 7-foot post spacing corresponds to a double 2 × 10, etc. This data is based upon the use of pressure-treated yellow pine.

Beams that are made up of three pieces of wood must be nailed or screwed together to take advantage of their combined strength.

Post height is a concern only when your deck is fairly tall. A 4-×-4 yellow pine post 8 feet tall will support any portion of the deck area up to 144 square feet. The load area is calculated by multiplying beam spacing by post spacing. In our example, we are supporting about 67 square feet with each post. Reading from the tables, our deck could be as high as 12 feet off the ground using a 4 × 4 of pressure-treated yellow pine.

If your deck bounces or seems like a diving board you better recalculate your supports, rebuilding is the only solution.

CONSTRUCTION PLAN LAYOUT

The first step in the construction of your patio or deck is a design or plan layout. If you are required to obtain a permit by your municipality, they will ask for a drawing of what you plan to construct. For a patio a *plan view*, looking down from above, will be enough to show your intent. There will be no additional structural concerns unless you are building a retaining wall to hold soil at an abrupt change in level. For a deck, elevations or side views will also be required. Your plan should show the foundation, posts, beams, joist, decking, railing, and stairs. The plan should show how the deck is fastened together, and the size and spacing of the members. A *site plan*, a drawing of your whole property, will usually be required to show how the project relates to the house and other structures as well as the property lines (Fig. 2-11).

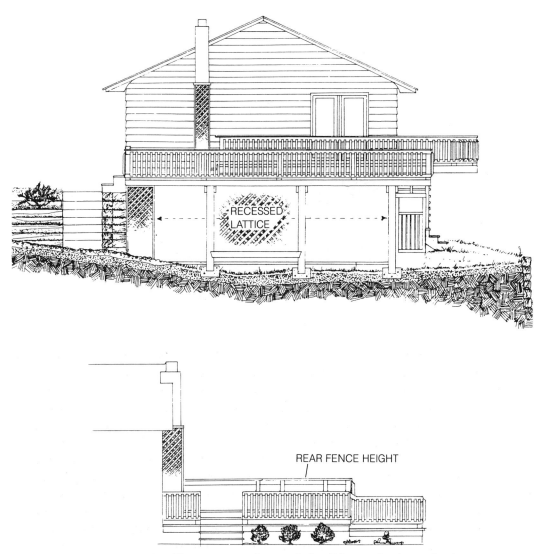

Fig. 2-11. People will want to see a layout of what it is you plan to construct.

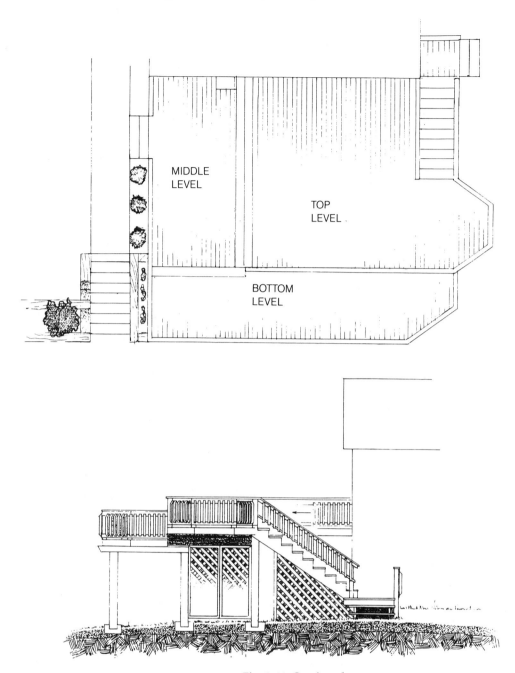

MIDDLE
LEVEL

TOP
LEVEL

BOTTOM
LEVEL

Fig. 2-11. Continued.

It might sound tedious and time consuming to do all of this planning and layout, but in the long run it will simplify the whole construction process. By first thinking through your project on paper, you will eliminate the costly errors that occur when you build "by the seat of your pants." You will speed up the building process because you know exactly what you are going to do. Finally, it will enable you to develop a bill of materials and cost out the project accurately. The following steps will help you on your way to building the project.

First, obtain some graph paper with $1/4$-inch grids. If the project is large, $1/8$-inch grids might be preferable. Each square or grid should equal one square foot. For purpose of this discussion, let us assume you are building a deck onto the back of your house. Start by measuring the existing wall of your house. It might have various ins and outs, jogs, and setbacks. These each should be measured and accurately drawn on the paper. Determine the size of the deck you wish to build and add it to the drawing in the correct location. If stairs are to be a part of the design, add them at this time. Staircases are normally 3 to 4 feet wide, but they can be any width you desire.

To calculate the length of the steps, measure from the top of the deck to the point on the ground where you think the steps will end. Convert this number to inches and divide by 7. Round off to the nearest whole number. This will give you the number of risers and steps for a 7-inch rise and an 11-inch run. (A very comfortable set of steps to walk.) Subtract 1 from the total to get the number of steps.

Example

Distance from deck to where steps will end = 5 feet and 2 inches or 62 inches total. Divide by 7 = 8.857. Round off to nearest whole number = 9 risers. Subtract 1 = 8 steps (Fig. 2-12).

In practice many combinations of rise and run are comfortable to walk. As a rule of thumb, the sum of the rise and run should equal 18 inches. By that rule, a rise of 4 inches and a run of 14 inches would be just as comfortable. Steeper steps are harder to climb, but a rise of 10 inches and a run of 8 inches would work just as well. The practical limit is reached when the tread is too small to fit your foot. The most important point is that each set of steps be equal in height. Variations in the step height could lead people to stumble and fall.

One more calculation is necessary to obtain the actual distance in each rise. To do this, divide the total distance (62 inches) by the number of risers (9). It should be near 7 inches, 6.889 inches, or just over $6^{7}/_{8}$ inches. Each tread will be about 11 inches front to back.

Going back to the outline you just made, start drawing in the elements of the deck in layers. Let your outline represent the decking and stairs. The next layer below that is the joists. Lay a piece of tracing paper over the basic outline, retrace the outline, then draw in the joists to scale at 16 or 24 inches apart. Make certain that you place a joist at each end of the deck. Use the grid of the original drawing to size and space the joist properly. All of the decking material that we will recommend can be used at either the 16- or 24-inch spacing.

At this point you have a choice to make in the location of the joists. If they are placed perpendicular to the house, the house wall might support one end resulting in some savings in lumber. If they are parallel to the house then they must be supported by two or more independent beams. Decking is usually applied perpendicular to the joists, which might influence the way in which you want to run the joists (Fig. 2-13).

The next step is the layout of the retaining walls or beams that support the joists. Take another piece of tracing paper and lay it on top of the joist drawing. Draw in the location of each supporting beam or wall. If you have elected to have the joists run out from the house, only one more supporting beam will be needed. Consult the joist span table to determine the size of the joists you will need to span the distance. If 2 × 12s will not make the span, you must add an intermediate beam. Doing so will often allow you to use a smaller joist so check the joist table again.

If you have chosen to run your joists parallel to the house, divide the total distance into spans that make sense when you consult the joist span table. You might choose your beam spacing based on the size of the joist you want to use or the beam spacing you want. Either will work.

When you have determined the number and spacing of your beams, draw them on a third layer of tracing paper. Keep this layer to add the posts or piers that will support the beam(s). Consult the beam table to determine the distance each post must be placed from each other. Consult the post size table to determine the proper post size to use. Larger cross sections are required for taller posts and greater loads.

The next step is to lay out the railings and railing posts. To do this, remove the overlays created for joists, beams, and posts. Lay another blank piece of tracing paper over your original outline. Draw in the railing post locations. To properly support a rail, there needs to be

STAIR AND RAMP RAILINGS

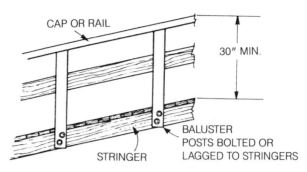

Cap and cross members should parallel stringers—posts should be truly vertical.

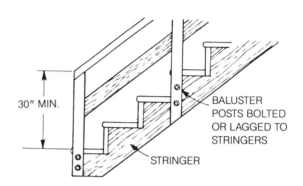

Lagged securely to stringers, stair and ramp railing posts should be in vertical position.

SUGGESTED RATIOS
RISERS & TREADS

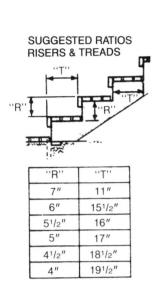

"R"	"T"
7"	11"
6"	15¹/₂"
5¹/₂"	16"
5"	17"
4¹/₂"	18¹/₂"
4"	19¹/₂"

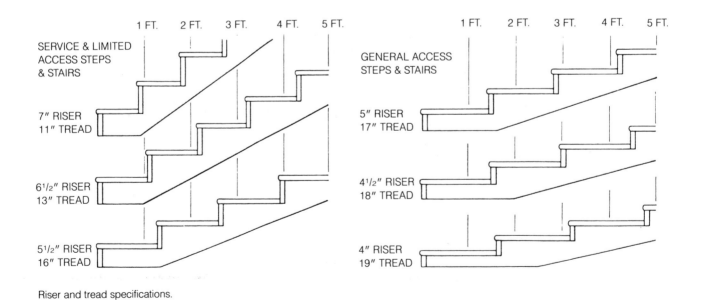

Riser and tread specifications.

Fig. 2-12. These are some typical combinations of rise and run in step and ramp construction.

Fig. 2-13. Joist hangers are the popular choice for adding a deck to an existing house.

a post at each corner and at each side of an opening. Draw in spaced posts between the corner and end posts. Any uniform spacing up to 8 feet is acceptable. The idea is to create a pleasing but structurally sound rail system.

According to most code standards, railing heights must be 36 inches when the deck is within 24 inches of the ground, and 42 inches above that. For the safety of babies and small children the largest spacing allowed between rails is 6 inches. Check with your local code.

Once you have determined all the posts, beams, joists, decking, and railing types and sizes you intend to use, you can easily make up a shopping list for your project. From this shopping list you can determine the price of your materials. Count up the size, length, and quantity of each item and enter it into your materials list.

ESTIMATING DECK MATERIALS FROM THE GROUND UP

- concrete
- reinforcing rods
- forming materials
- post anchors
- posts
- beam saddles or other steel tie materials
- bolts to attach the beam to the post
- beam lumber
- joist lumber
- hurricane ties
- joist hangers or other joist tie material
- nails or screws for joists

- stringers for stairs
- bolts for stringers
- decking and stair tread
- nails or screws for decking and stairs
- railing posts
- other railing lumber
- bolts for railing
- nails or screws for railing

Estimating the time to complete your project is another matter. There are too many variables including skill level, preplanning, hours worked per day, etc. that will be the final determining factor. Remember to allow time for inspections. If you are working on the weekends you might have to dig holes for piers on one Saturday, have the inspection done during the week, and then pour the concrete the next Saturday.

TOOLS USED IN DECK CONSTRUCTION

A deck can be constructed entirely with hand tools or with a combination of both hand tools and power tools. The lists in this section will give you some idea of the recommended tools to make the project go quickly and with a minimum of effort.

Hand Tools

- hammer (16 oz. or 20 oz.)
- saw (rip and crosscut and a backsaw for appearance cuts)
- drill (standard or brace and bit)
- chisel
- plane
- chalk line
- wrenches (box, open end, adjustable, vise grips)
- shovel
- post-hole digger
- masons trowel
- framing square
- masons twine
- tape measure

Power Tools

- drill (preferably a cordless 9.6- to 12-volt variable speed with reverse. This can not only drill the holes but allow fast assembly with screws, drill bits, and screwdriver bit.)

- circular saw (7$^1/_2$-inch carbide blade)

- miter saw with compound cutting angle

- portable radial arm saw

- portable table saw

- reciprocating saw with 8-inch fine tooth blade

- router and bits for shaping applications

- band saw or sabre saw for curve cuts

- nail gun

3

Deck Construction

SITE PREPARATION

IT IS TIME TO BUILD THE DECK. HOPEFULLY YOU HAVE SQUARED YOUR DREAMS TO YOUR POCK-etbook and have settled on a design that will be strong, secure, and beautiful. By now, you have checked on the location of all underground utilities and have protected the planting you want to save. You have the tools and the materials all at hand. It is time to put the shovel to earth.

Using your drawings, locate the positions of the concrete piers or walls on the ground. Drive a stake into the center point for each pier. String lines drawn over the center of each pier will help you align and position the piers and also the post anchors after the concrete is poured. Remember, your entire deck will be built on this foundation; accuracy counts.

If your foundation is piers, dig them 12 inches in diameter to the depth based upon your local building code, probably between 24 and 36 inches. Bell them out at the bottom to about 14 to 16 inches. Install short pieces of round cardboard-forming tube or build a 12-inch square form out of 1-×-8 stock. Allow the pier to extend about 8 inches above the ground. Call for your ground inspection (Fig. 3-1).

After your approval to proceed, pour the concrete into the forms. Before the concrete sets, restring the lines over the piers to locate the center of the post anchors (Fig. 3-2). Push the post anchors firmly into the wet concrete. Concrete takes 28 days to cure and to gain its full strength, so be careful when you start to set the posts the next day.

If you are building a wall to support your deck, you will need to dig a continuous trench instead of individual holes in the ground for footings. The trench should be at least 16 inches wide and dug to the depth required for your area. You are going to make the wall in two sections, the footing and the foundation. These are made with two separate pourings of concrete. Call for your ground inspection.

After the inspection pour the concrete level with the top of the footing form. Install rebar (steel reinforcing rods) into the concrete. One method of assuring strong connections between the footing and the foundations is to drag the corner of a board down the center of the concrete the length of the footing or base about an inch deep. This will act as a keyway to lock the footing and the foundation together.

To form your foundation wall, you will need to build a hollow wall form to contain the concrete (Fig. 3-3). This can be made from 3/4-inch plywood or you can rent forms for this purpose. Make certain the walls are supported properly to take the weight of the concrete. Build the forms slightly taller than the desired wall height. Snap a level chalkline on the

Fig. 3-1. A post-hole digger will quicken the job of creating piers.

SETTING COLUMNS OR POSTS

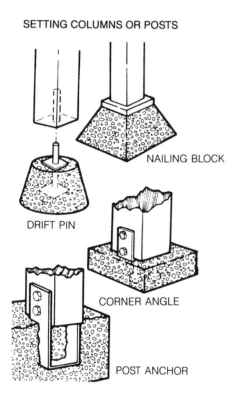

NAILING BLOCK

DRIFT PIN

CORNER ANGLE

POST ANCHOR

There are several ways to connect post to footings.
It is easier to place anchors before concrete sets.

EMBEDDING COLUMNS OR POSTS

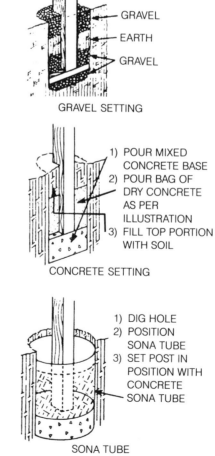

GRAVEL

EARTH

GRAVEL

GRAVEL SETTING

1) POUR MIXED CONCRETE BASE
2) POUR BAG OF DRY CONCRETE AS PER ILLUSTRATION
3) FILL TOP PORTION WITH SOIL

CONCRETE SETTING

1) DIG HOLE
2) POSITION SONA TUBE
3) SET POST IN POSITION WITH CONCRETE

SONA TUBE

SONA TUBE

Fig. 3-2. Post setting methods.

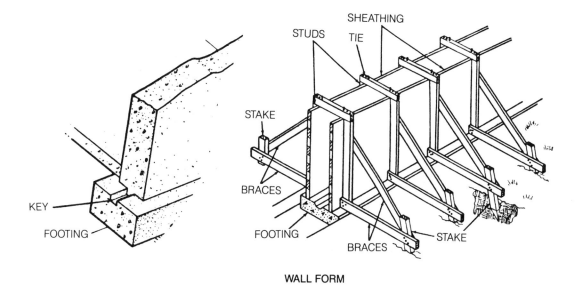

Fig. 3-3. Pouring wall foundation.

inside of the form to indicate the pourline. It is important to add two No. 4 rebars ($1/2''$) at the top and bottom of any wall to add to the strength of the wall. This must be done as you pour the concrete.

Concrete can be purchased in wet or dry form. You can mix your own or order premix. Truck delivery of premix is desirable when the amount needed is over one cubic yard. Material yards prefer to deliver a minimum of three cubic yards, and you might have to pay a premium for a lesser amount.

When pouring concrete, it is important to not let one section harden before pouring the next. If you do, a cold joint will result, which weakens the wall.

If you decide to mix the concrete yourself, premix bags that weigh about 80 pounds will make about a $2/3$-cubic foot of concrete. This is the easy way to do it. If you need to mix larger amounts you will have to buy the raw materials. If so, obtain them in the ratio of 1:2:3. That is, one part cement to two parts sand, and three parts gravel. Add water to this mixture to make a paste or plastic consistency. The mix should be uniform.

Regardless of how you obtain the concrete, pour it to the chalkline in the forms and level it. Set anchor bolts into the wet concrete at each end and at 4-foot intervals. Bolts (J-bolts) are used to anchor a wood sill plate to the top of the wall so make certain you leave them sticking up 3 or 4 inches.

FRAMING

After the piers or walls have been poured you can begin to assemble the deck framing. There are specific terms for the various parts of deck framing. We will describe each part, its use, and the alternatives for fastening it to the other members of the deck structure (Fig. 3-4).

On piers, the next members are usually *posts*. The posts are wooden uprights usually 4 × 4s, 4 × 6s, or 6 × 6s. The posts support the beams or stringers above (Fig. 3-5). The posts should fit snugly into the post anchors. Drive galvanized nails or preferably treated screws through the holes in the sides of the anchor to hold the post in place.

One note about hardware and fasteners is important at this point. All of these items should be rustproof. Your deck will be ruined with stains from the hardware over a period of years if the hardware has not had the proper treatment. While we reference nails for deck

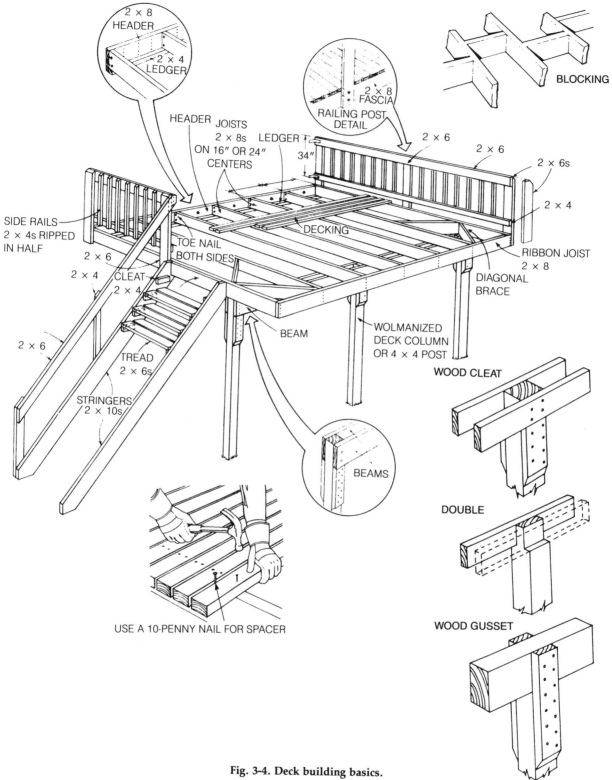

Fig. 3-4. Deck building basics.

Fig. 3-5. Posts on piers.

construction, screws are the preferred fastener. Nails tend to pop up after a period of time and have to be renailed (Fig. 3-6).

Beams or stringers are placed on top of the posts. These will support the joists. A beam is fastened to the top of the post with metal T-straps or saddles. Use screws that are at least 2¹/₂ inches long (Fig. 3-7). Stringers, another form of a beam, are fastened to the side of a post. The strongest method is to mount the stringer into a notch cut into the top side of the post. In any event the fastener of choice is ¹/₂-inch carriage bolts. Predrill holes in both the post and stringer and install the bolt with large flat washers (Fig. 3-8).

In the case of a wall foundation, a sill plate, normally a 2 × 4 or 2 × 6 is the equivalent of the beam or stringer. This is fastened to the foundation with bolts set in the concrete. It will support the joists that are fastened to the sill plate (Fig. 3-9).

Joists are the next layer on the deck. The joists will support the decking. They are normally placed 16 to 24 inches apart on either the sill plate, beam, or stringer. They are fastened down with hurricane ties or cross nailing, or they are hung between the beams with the use of joist hangers. Joists come in 2 × 6s, 2 × 8s, 2 × 10s, and 2 × 12s (Figs. 3-10 through 3-12).

Wall plates the same size as the joist lumber are used to attach joists to the side of a wall

Fig. 3-6 and 3-7. Nails will hold facing boards okay, but lag screws must be used for joist support.

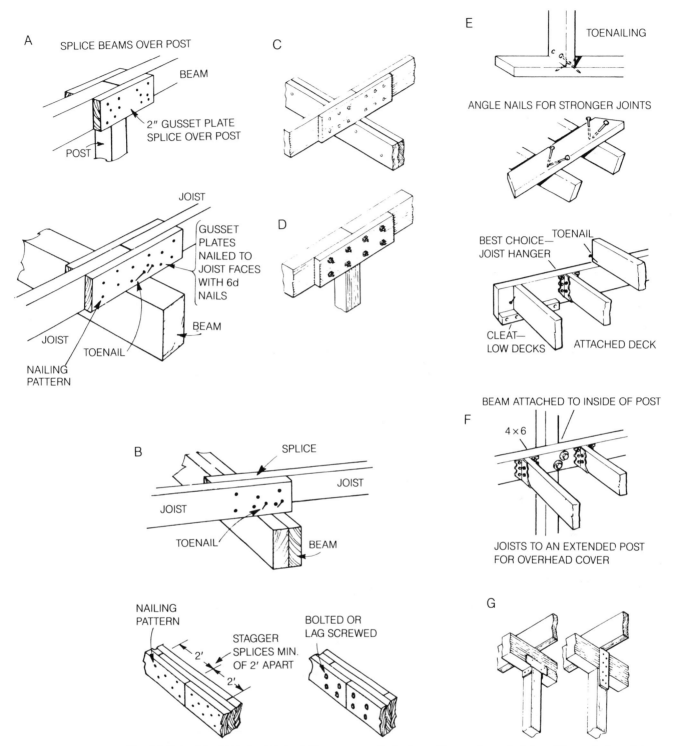

Fig. 3-8. Joist Attachments. (A) use 16d common nails for toenailing and gusset plate nailing or fasten plate with bolts or lag screws; **(B)** 2″ lumber spliced to form a 6″ beam, nail at 2′ intervals on both faces with 6d common galv. nails or bolt or lag screw both sides of each splice; **(C)** use a butt joint over post and tie the two beams together by fastening a cleat to each side to achieve additional length; **(D)** for thicker joist beams, build them up from thinner members by fastening pieces together with bolts or lag screws; **(E)** joists attach to ledger with a cleat, joist hanger, or toenailed on top; **(F)** use joist hangers to attach beams to a post that also supports overhead cover or a railing; **(G)** to fasten beams to top of posts, use cleats and metal connectors.

Fig. 3-9. A sill plate (board) is anchored to the concrete wall or foundation.

Fig. 3-10. Joists are the next layer on the deck.

Fig. 3-11. Joists support the decking.

Fig. 3-12. A secondary joist is layed to provide a second level.

or house. Lag screws (¹/₂-inch) should be used for this purpose for wood structures or ¹/₂-inch expansion bolts for a masonry structure (Fig. 3-13).

Railing posts should be installed at this time so they can extend through the decking. They should be bolted to the joist structure using at least ¹/₂-inch carriage or machine bolts (Fig. 3-14). Railing posts are usually 4 × 4s, but other lumber sizes can be used for variety.

Blocking is a stabilizer placed between the joists to keep them from twisting under load. When the joists have free spans of over 8 feet, blocking is installed midspan. Blocking can be made from short pieces of the joist material or from 1-×-4 material installed in an X pattern or metal cross bridging.

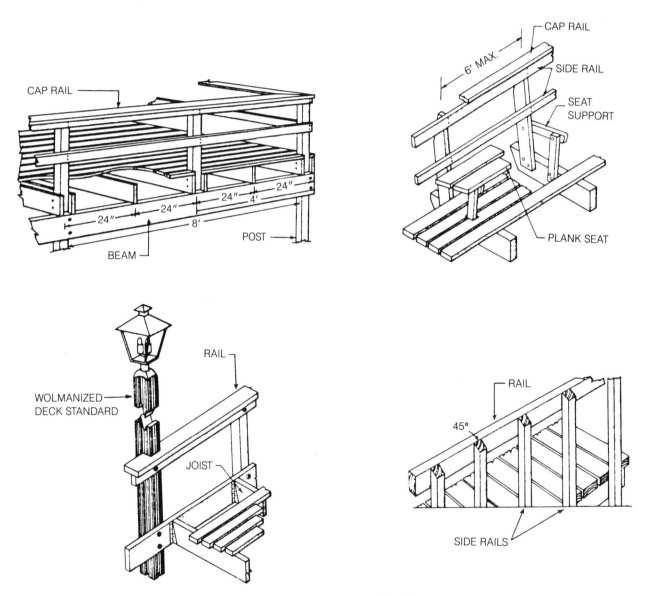

Fig. 3-13. These are some railing ideas.

Fig. 3-14. Carriage bolts are the preferred choice for holding railing posts.

LAYING THE DECKING

This is the creative aspect of building a deck. There are many decking patterns that can be installed that will add to the appearance of your project. There are, however, three rules, each piece of decking must end with support from a joist or solid blocking. Solid decking requires a pitched joist system to allow water to run away from the house. The decking should always be placed heartwood side down (Fig. 3-15).

The most straightforward style of decking is boards laid side-by-side perpendicular to the joists (Fig. 3-16). This is the quickest and easiest to install and uses the least amount of material. If you are installing spaced decking, keep it under 1/2 inch, as anything wider will be hazardous for chair legs and narrow heels. Experienced deck builders use a 16-penny nail or a carpenter's pencil for a spacer (Fig. 3-17). As you install the decking, measure the distance to the far side frequently. Adjust your spacing as needed to keep this distance even.

Tongue and groove planking is normally installed the same way except the boards are run perpendicular to the house so the water runs along their entire length. Water will collect in the cracks and behind cupped boards if the boards and the pitch do not run the same way.

Another popular style is diagonal or bias decking. This will work well for either spaced or solid decking. It is easiest to install all the boards leaving the ends hanging raggedly off the edge of the deck (Fig. 3-18). Afterwards you can mark a straight line and then cut the board ends even.

More complicated styles of decking do not work well with tongue and groove, but do with spaced decking. Spaced decking is usually 2 × 4s or 2 × 6s. These smaller widths are less subject to warping and cupping than wider boards. They are also easier to manipulate for uniform spacing. Remember that there is always more waste with complicated patterns of decking, but the results can be quite eye-pleasing and worth the effort and investment.

Nails have been the traditional fastener of choice for decking. Nails unfortunately tend to pop up after awhile. A new screw product has been introduced that solves that problem

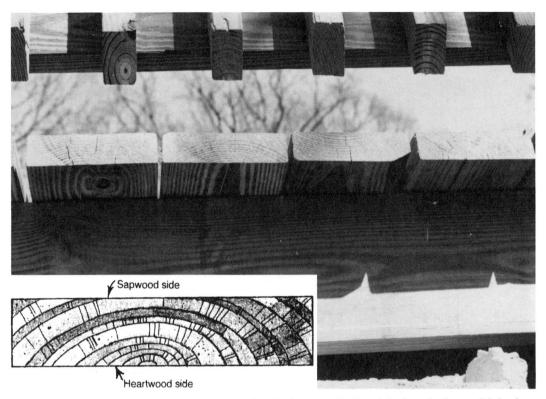

Sapwood side

Heartwood side

Fig. 3-15. Deckboards should always be layed with the heartwood side of the boards down. Of the four board ends shown here, which one was installed incorrectly?

Fig. 3-16. This is the most common pattern for deckboards.

Fig. 3-17. A 16d nail is sufficient to space deckboards.

Fig. 3-18. Leave the boards hanging over the end then cut flush after they are nailed in place.

permanently. These are slotted Phillips-headed screws that are specially treated and have a self-tapping action that recesses the screw head into the wood when driven with a power drill or screwdriver.

Bias-radius decking is a product that is one-inch thick and has rounded edges that produce a more polished looking deck. You can achieve this same look with the use of a router and a quarter-round bit. This could enhance the appearance of not only the decking but also the railing and railing posts.

If you plan to deck around your favorite tree, remember trees grow. You will have to modify your joist system to fit around a tree properly. Joists must be boxed-off using doubled members and joist hangers on all sides of the tree.

DECK RAILING TYPES

There are many options and choices for deck railing types (Figs. 3-19, 3-20). However, current building standards require a maximum spacing between railing members of at least 6 inches. This is considered small enough to prevent the head of a baby from passing through. This requirement, where enforced, has limited the options for deck railing types. We suggest that you check with your local building inspector to see what the code requires.

The old standard porch railing is still an attractive option (Fig. 3-21). It has a molded cap and base rail with spaced pickets in between. Another option is to run a 2-×-4 top rail even with the joists and then attach 2 × 2s with mitered ends to the toprail and joist (Figs. 3-22 through 3-24).

Fig. 3-19. The spacing for railing is normally 6 inches.

Fig. 3-20. Check with your local code for spacing of railing.

Fig. 3-21. This is a nice form of railing and is made from split 2 × 4s.

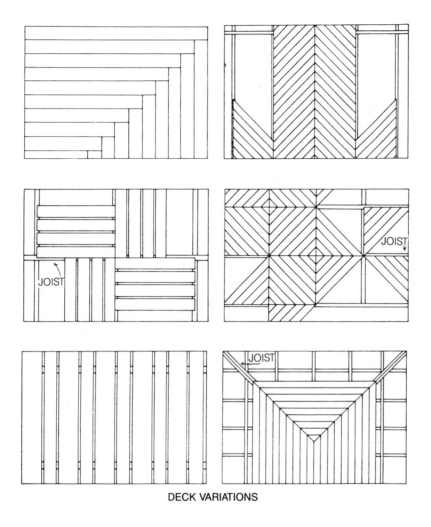

DECK VARIATIONS

SCREENING VARIATIONS

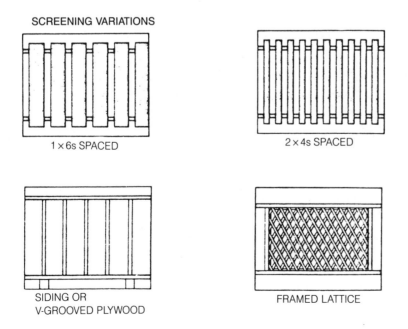

1 × 6s SPACED

2 × 4s SPACED

SIDING OR
V-GROOVED PLYWOOD

FRAMED LATTICE

Fig. 3-22. Deck and screen variations.

Today's decks and patios are the modern-day version of the old-fashioned back porch. With the availability of modern materials and techniques, the options for appearance, size, and function are enormous.

This high-rise deck allows its occupants a superb view of the surrounding area. The height of this type of deck requires proper sizing of the supporting columns and bracing, extremely important factors for stability.

This deck is completely outfitted with matching lattice chaise lounge, chair, and barbeque. The picnic table is convenient for outdoor dining.

Deck designs are limited only by imagination, as shown in this view. The upper level of this high-rise deck is multisided and provides access to a second-story doorway.

Rather than clearing your lot of trees, consider integrating them into your deck design. The result is both attractive and practical, providing beauty and shade.

The sloping hillside presented its owners with challenges and opportunities for creating a unique deck design. The result here is a multilevel deck that is naturally shaded and provides an ideal intimate setting for entertaining.

A wood divider forms a decorative barrier against sun and wind and creates privacy. This option is particularly appealing for neighborhoods where the houses are built close together.

This simple concrete patio is inexpensive, easy to build, and creates an enjoyable outdoor sitting area.

Making your own deck furniture is much more rewarding than buying premade furnishings—and it will save you money, too. This rocking sling chair is comfortable, easy to make, and unique—it won't look like all the other deck chairs on the block.

This planter bench uses standard outdoor-furniture cushions and is made out of 2-×-4-inch material. The L-shaped design creates a cozy conversation nook.

Additional deck furniture includes these lattice chairs that complement the planter bench. The chairs are made from Wolmanized water-resistant, pressure-treated lumber for durability and protection from the elements.

The bench and tables with charming cut-out heart patterns were constructed from lumber scraps left over from the deck project.

When planning a deck, be sure that the materials you use complement those used on your existing home. The design shown is a good example of how you can integrate deck, house, and natural landscape.

This deck, surrounded by lush vegetation, extends your living space for dining and entertaining. This space-board covering and trees provide just the right amount of shade.

Unlike larger decks designed for entertaining groups of people, this charming deck off the master bedroom is perfect for two.

Even a small deck at the entryway can enhance the look of your home. This design is ideal for homes on small lots with little or no yard.

It is crucial that a deck be built strong enough to withstand all the normal pressure it will receive. Be sure to take into account the weight of the deck itself, the furniture and the people on it, and the forces of nature. The deck in this picture is supported by brick piers.

This lattice covering is an effective sun screen that looks good, too. It is especially well suited for homes that have little or no natural shading.

Raised decks are perfect for homes having a floor level that is more than one step above ground. A deck with steps makes a perfect transition from the ground level to your doorstep.

Still an attractive option, this old standard porch railing has a molded cap and base rail with spaced pickets. The spacing adheres to building codes designed to protect babies and small children from getting stuck between the pickets.

In designing a handrail for steps, it is customary to continue the design of the porch railing. The hand-rail should follow the angle of the step stringers.

A terraced patio can add a varied visual interest to your backyard. Because few sites are totally level, it is easier to construct a patio that follows the natural lay of the land.

By building steps to reach each new patio, you create an interesting multilevel effect.

Combining different materials for patios, steps, and walkways creates an interesting variety of colors, textures, and patterns that complements the natural landscape.

Railroad ties used for steps and retaining walls add a rustic touch and create a natural planter.

This wooden-and-stone walkway provides transition from a patio built on a steep hillside. This construction offers an attractive solution for problem landscapes.

Stone is a variable medium available in rich colors and textures. It is an ideal ''found'' material.

A deck with more than one level allows adults and children to have their own separate areas, while still being in view of one another.

No backyard is complete without a swing. Anchored to the bottom of the deck, this design is a new twist on the old-fashioned porch swing.

A plus with high-rise decks is the space created underneath, which can be used as a child's play area.

Low-voltage lighting systems such as these shaded tier lights provide plenty of light at a low cost. Easy to install, they are available at most home improvement centers. An added plus: Because you can keep them lit all night long, without receiving an astronomical utility bill at the end of the month, they add an element of security to your home.

Proper lighting transforms a sun deck into an ideal area for nighttime entertaining.

Fig. 3-23. A mitered end rail makes a nice appearance.

Fig. 3-24. A tapered end provides a nice design and provides an even flow of the rail line to the next level.

STEPS AND BANISTERS

Stringers are the basic supporting member for stairs (Fig. 3-25). The stringers can be cut to receive the steps or the steps can fit in between uncut stringers supported by metal or wood braces. Cut stringers must be made from 2-×-12 stock, a 2 × 10 might suffice for braced steps. Treads or steps longer than 3 feet will require a center support.

Select good solid straight lumber for stair stringers. Lay out the placement of the steps on the stringers (Fig. 3-26). Refer to chapter 2 to calculate the rise of each step. The run will be determined by the size of the board you will use (Fig. 3-27). If you use a 2 × 10, your run will be 9^1/$_4$ inch for each step. Two 2 × 6s with a small space will give a 11^1/$_4$-inch step. A framing square is indispensable for stringer layout (Fig. 3-28). Special stops are available to clamp onto the square to make each step precisely the same. Other jigs and fixtures can be purchased that allow you to use a router to carve a rabbet joint into which the step can also fit. Precision is important on a set of steps. Each riser and tread must stay constant in size. The step or tread must be level from side-to-side and front-to-back.

In designing a handrail for the steps it is customary to continue the design of the deck railing (Fig. 3-29). The handrail should follow the angle of the step stringers. The most comfortable height is 30 inches from the nose of the step. Taller rails might be required by local code (Fig. 3-30).

Fig. 3-25. Stringers are the basic supporting members for stairs.

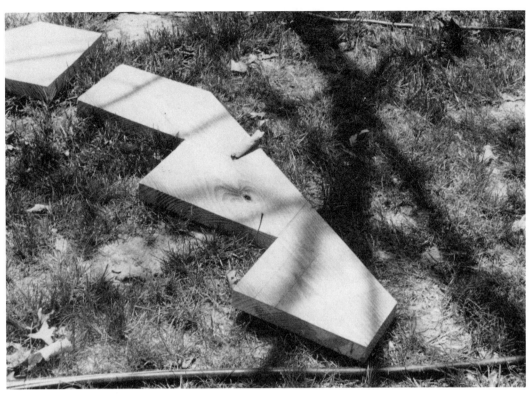

Fig. 3-26. Short stringers are needed for the steps off the landing and into the yard.

Fig. 3-27. Small cavities are dug into the ground to provide a foundation for the step stringers.

Fig. 3-28. Concrete is poured around and under the stringers to provide stability and support.

Fig. 3-29 and 3-30. Posts for step railing should be attached with carriage bolts and follow the contour of the step incline.

Fig. 3-30.

Fig. 3-31. The front of the finished deck disguises the extent of the deck's size and versatility.

Fig. 3-32. The back reveals the size and extent of the decks charm and its versatility.

Fig. 3-33. The lattice covers the storage area and hides the air conditioner housed under the steps.

Fig. 3-34. Looking down from above, the size and flexibility of the deck is more apparent.

CONNECTING DECKS

To connect decks built at two different heights requires either steps or a ramp as a connector. To build steps between two decks is the same as building steps from the ground level. Measure the difference in each deck's height. For example, a deck of 48 inches and a deck of 70 inches would have a difference of 22 inches. Dividing by 3 would give you a rise of 7.33 inches for each step. If the two decks are two feet apart, you can use two 12-inch steps. If the distance is further, you might want to use wider steps or divide the distance into 4 rises.

Building a ramp between two decks requires the same kind of framing as the decking. It requires properly spaced and sized joists. Since inclined surfaces are likely to be hazardous, we suggest you use 1-×-1 cleats or friction strips along the ramp surface.

When connecting decks are at the same level, the connector is called a *bridge* or *catwalk*. The same building principles as decking apply (Figs. 3-31 through 3-34).

4

Patios and
Walkway Construction

SITE PREPARATION

PATIO CONSTRUCTION IS SIGNIFICANTLY MORE FLEXIBLE THAN DECK CONSTRUCTION. WITHout the constraints of structural considerations, you are free to create an outdoor space equal to the limits of your imagination and pocket book. You will find that your most creative ideas can really come alive with a wide range of possibilities that your land may offer. You will have an unlimited source of construction products, plants, shrubs, trees, bushes and both paid for and found materials to select from.

You can fit your patio into the natural shape of your site or you can rearrange the landscape to offer intimate nooks or wide open spaces. You can cut your patio into the side of a hill by placing terrace gardens above it or by building a retaining wall. You can build-up the land to create the perfect level or multilevel site for your patio. You can integrate existing trees, structures, and joint multiple-outdoor living areas with stepways and walkways. All-in-all, patios have it over decks when it comes to flexibility and options.

There are three essential factors to consider when preparing the site for your new patio: proper drainage, stable base, and a proper foundation. Without all three you cannot create a successful patio.

Proper drainage is essential to any patio. Your patio will be useable more quickly after a storm if the water can run off harmlessly. In areas where freezing temperatures are attained in the winter, good drainage is particularly important because of the damaging effects of ice. Another problem related to drainage is erosion. Large nonporous surfaces can funnel a great volume of water to a new location in your yard. Be prepared to handle this influx of water, protecting your soil with plantings or terracing that will slow the water and allow it to soak into the ground without doing damage. A slope of 1/4 inch per foot on your patio surface will give good drainage without giving you that uncomfortable feeling that too much slope can give (Fig. 4-1).

The base of your patio, the layer beneath the patio surface, must be of proper materials. The durability of your patio and the beauty of the finished patio surface is determined by the quality of the base material supporting it. Base materials are compacted dirt, sand, rock, and concrete. The most successful bases for brick, paved, and stone patios are rock and concrete, which are the most stable. Sand, gravel, or compacted limestone with small fine particles in it also will do if it is packed to a thickness of 4 to 6 inches. This is especially true if

Fig. 4-1. Good drainage can be obtained by a ¹/₄-inch drop per one foot of patio length.

you plan to use appearance stones for a walkway since they will be quickly pushed into the mud after a rain without the base (Fig. 4-2). Remember to allow for the slope for drainage.

A foundation is sometimes necessary with patio construction as well as deck construction. Some situations that call for a foundation include:

■ Patios on a steep hillside (Fig. 4-3)

■ Retaining walls in conjunction with a patio

■ Base for brick walls or edgers

■ Patios that will have additional structures on top

■ Patios that cannot be subject to freeze/thaw movement

Fig. 4-2. Appearance stones can be quickly added to a walkway and enhance the entrance to a deck or patio.

Fig. 4-3. This is a unique combination of flag stones, decking, appearance stones, and railroad ties retaining concrete on a steep hillside.

A foundation for a patio is no different than for any other structure. While there are many different forms of foundations we will only address the use of poured concrete in this section.

Foundations take the form of walls and piers. Foundation walls will support much more force than a pier, both straight down and laterally. Piers offer more than enough support for and protection for the freeze/thaw movement and to support light structures such as a screen house on the patio. When a foundation is being constructed along with a concrete slab, it is often possible to pour both the footing and the slab at the same time. See the illustrations in this chapter for more details.

Sometimes building a patio requires the movement of a great deal of earth. Renting a Bobcat or similar device will speed up the preparation. If a lot of earth has to be moved it is better to hire an experienced excavation contractor.

DESIGNING AND SHAPING YOUR PATIO

Planning a patio is the same as planning a deck. You have to develop the construction plan layout. Use graph paper to lay out the location of your house and the patio as it relates to your house and the other structures nearby. Locate power and telephone lines and trees and show them on your layout. As previously described in the construction plan layout section, let each square represent one square foot. Show any paths, steps, level changes, retaining walls, and plantings that you intend to install. The time you spend planning will make the actual construction task much easier. Think about the tasks that you must do and the sequence in order to complete the tasks of building the patio project. Make a list of all the tools and materials you will need. This plan will be required if you are building in an area that requires permits before construction can begin.

The design possibilities with materials for patios is endless. Wonderful patterns can be arranged with bricks alone. By combining materials, the multitude of textures and combinations give you many options to consider in your patio designs (Figs. 4-4, 4-5). Imagine a patio of brick pavers with cobblestone edgers, railroad tie steps, and terracing with bark walkways ringed with tasteful plantings. This is indeed a marvelous feast for the eyes. Look for ideas in this book and around your neighborhood, don't be afraid to dream up something unique for yourself.

Where decks are naturally angular, patios can be flowing, freeform shapes. Where decks have to be built to structural standards, patios rely on the ground for support. Where deck materials must be naturally or chemically treated to prevent the ravages of nature, patio materials are nearly always built of the earth and nature.

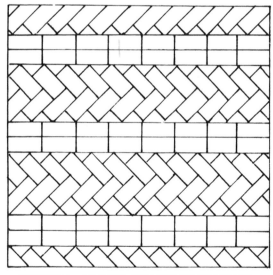

DIAGONAL · JACK ON JACK AND HERRINGBONE

Fig. 4-4 and 4-5. Patio designs are shown on pages 64 and 65.

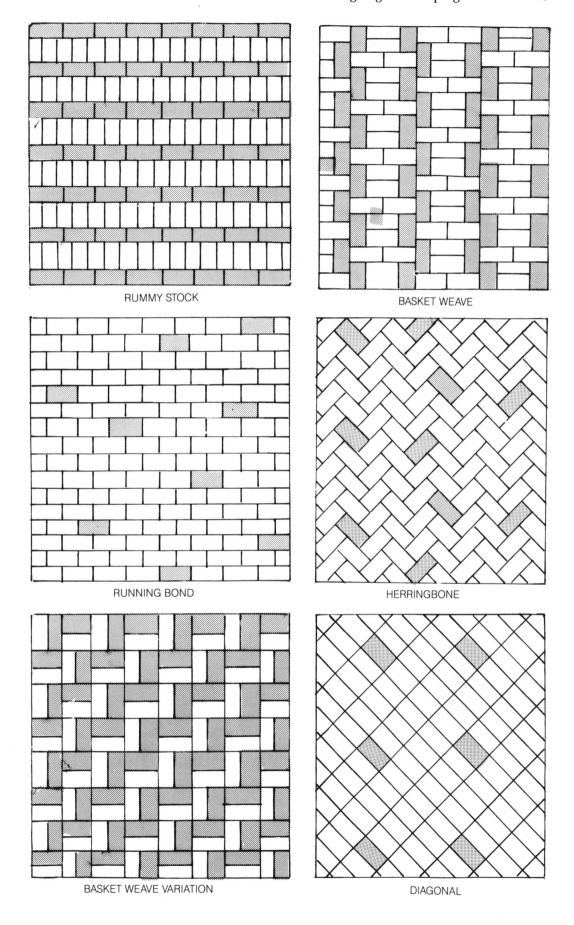

RUMMY STOCK

BASKET WEAVE

RUNNING BOND

HERRINGBONE

BASKET WEAVE VARIATION

DIAGONAL

SELECTION OF CONSTRUCTION MATERIALS

Concrete is the most common patio material. Concrete can be formed into any shape and is very strong, especially when reinforced with steel rods or mesh. Concrete can be colored before or after pouring. It can be finished rough or smooth or have exposed aggregate in its surface; its surface, which is long-lasting, can be made to look like brick or stone. When compared to brick or stone patios, it is much faster to install, is less expensive, and easier to work with. Concrete is also the product of choice as a stable base for other paving materials (Figs. 4-6, 4-7).

Wood can be integrated with concrete and other paving materials. Railroad ties, heart

Fig. 4-6. Plain concrete with proper landscaping and shrubbery can make a comfortable outdoor setting.

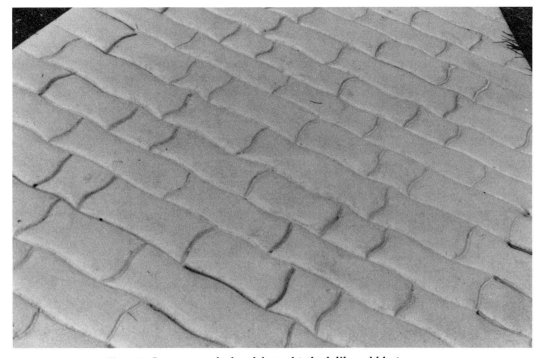

Fig. 4-7. Concrete can be hand formed to look like cobblestones.

redwood, and pressure-treated lumber are the only wood products that can be expected to last. Wood can be used as forms, expansion joints, or dividers for mixtures of patio materials. In addition, wood pallets can be made to lay on the ground. Interesting patterns can be formed by laying the pallets at right angles to one another (Fig. 4-8). Wood products such as bark or wood chips are used for paths and wear areas under children's play equipment. They work equally well for mulching garden areas as well. Wood 2 × 4 s and 2 × 6s can be kerfed and bent and used as edgers for patios as well as walkways (Fig. 4-9).

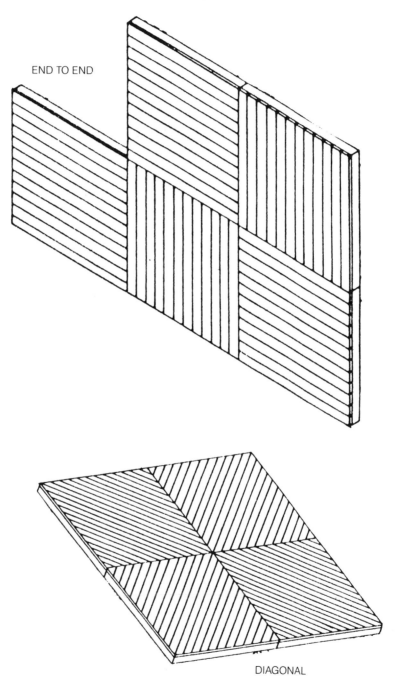

Fig. 4-8. Wood pallets can be quickly made to lay on the ground, interesting patterns can be formed by laying the pallets at right angles to one another.

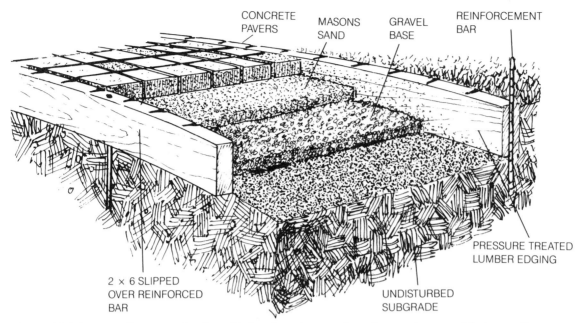

CONCRETE
PAVERS

MASONS
SAND

GRAVEL
BASE

REINFORCEMENT
BAR

PRESSURE TREATED
LUMBER EDGING

2 × 6 SLIPPED
OVER REINFORCED
BAR

UNDISTURBED
SUBGRADE

Fig. 4-9. This is an excellent example of wood being shaped to contain various paving materials for a walkway.

Other materials suited for paths and garden treatments are rocks and stone. Small river gravel or crushed limestone can make a charming patio area such as under a tree where grass won't grow (Fig. 4-10). These materials must have edgers to contain them or they will spread beyond the intended area.

The most impressive patio product is brick. Brick is the patio material that says "class" and "quality." Bricks are available in a wide range of sizes and colors from white through

Fig. 4-10. This is a unique combination of edgers, pavers, and crushed rock.

yellows, browns, and red to nearly black. Their uniformity makes them easy to lay accurately. Many patterns are possible using the rectangular variety (Fig. 4-11).

Stone is a variable medium available in rich colors and textures. Stone takes a lot of patience to lay because of the size variations and the random shapes, but the results can be glorious (Fig. 4-12). Some of the many stones available include limestone (flagstone), sandstone, granite, and slate. Stone is the ideal found-material and might be as available as your nearest highway construction project or river bed.

Paving blocks, like brick, are a uniform patio material. They are usually made from concrete or fired clay. Concrete pavers are available in a wide range of shapes and sizes. Some fired clay pavers come in fairly complicated interlocking shapes in addition to square, rectangular, hexagonal, and other shapes.

Fig. 4-11. This combination of bricks and treated lumber retainers says first class.

Fig. 4-12. Limestone walkways such as this can be made from found materials and make elegant additions to your backyard.

CONCRETE PATIO CONSTRUCTION

A concrete patio can be installed in three ways, slab on grade, slab on piers, or slab on foundation. These three ways represent the most common form of concrete patio formation. *Slab on grade* is merely concrete sitting on the ground. Control joints are very important because the concrete will move and crack over the years. Control joints don't stop the cracking, they merely make it happen where you want it to happen. *Piers* are columns of concrete below the slab that stabilize the slab in the event of wash-out or earth movements. Foundations can afford a good deal of stability to the slab, but the work and cost involved can add considerably to the cost of construction.

I assume at this point you now have laid out your plan, acquired the permit, prepared the base for your patio. Now, you are breathlessly waiting for the remainder of the instructions.

The *formwork* is the container that holds the concrete in place while it sets up. Let's pour a 4-inch thick patio slab. Formwork for a 4-inch slab is normally made with 2 × 4s set up ¹/₂ inch from the ground. Nail the 2 × 4s to stakes driven into the ground at two foot intervals on the outside of the 2 × 4 forming boards. Fill in a little dirt or sand beneath the 2 × 4 to prevent the concrete from escaping. For cement requirements, see Figs. 4-13 and 4-14.

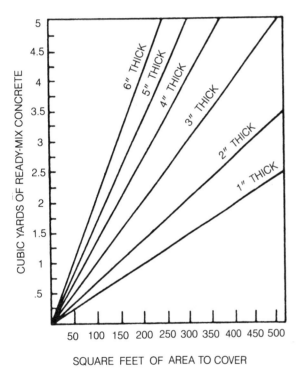

Fig. 4-13. This chart shows the formula for calculating your concrete requirements for your patio project.

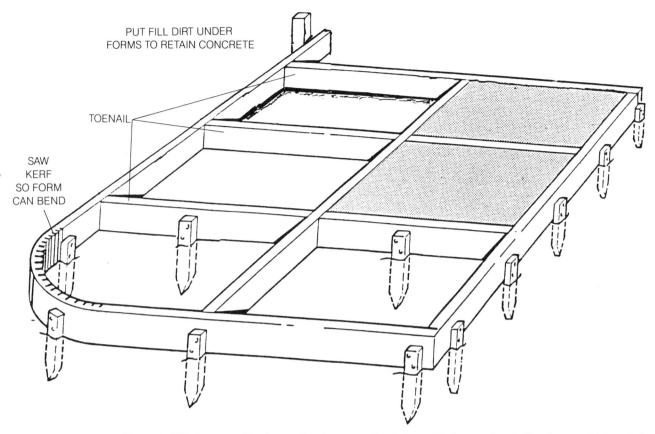

PUT FILL DIRT UNDER
FORMS TO RETAIN CONCRETE

TOENAIL

SAW
KERF
SO FORM
CAN BEND

Fig. 4-14. This is an excellent example of pressure treated wood being used as both a form and integrated with the concrete to form the patio design.

If your design calls for a curved edge to your patio, try either a kerfed 1 × 4 or ¹/₄ inch Masonite to form the curve. Kerfing involves cutting the 1 × 4 ¹/₂ to ⁵/₈ inches deep at ¹/₂ inch intervals along the entire length of the board to be bent to the curve. If the wood is free of knots the remaining wood will not break as you bend the curve. We recommend that you fasten the kerfed board to stakes with screws to prevent the shock of nailing (Fig. 4-15). Use preboring/self-drilling screws.

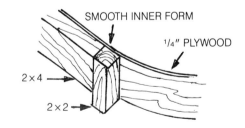

SMOOTH INNER FORM

¹/₄" PLYWOOD

2 × 4

2 × 2

Fig. 4-15. Thin plywood can be bent to form corners and retain the wet concrete. Support is needed at one-foot intervals to provide adequate strength.

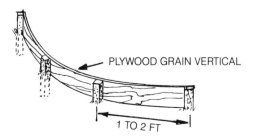

PLYWOOD GRAIN VERTICAL

1 TO 2 FT

Control joints can be made by installing redwood or pressure-treated 1 × 4s at intervals of ten feet or less (Fig. 4-16). You can interlock the boards by cutting ³/₄-inch slots halfway through each board so they will interlock at each joint location rather than using shorter pieces of wood to form patterns (Fig. 4-17). Striking a joint with a jointing tool requires good timing. The concrete must be hard enough to support your weight on kneeling boards, but soft enough to take the joint. I have seen control joints made with standard expansion joint material as well as railroad ties.

Where additional strength is desired you can install welded wire mesh into your slab (Fig. 4-18). This will not prevent cracking but will hold the pieces together and probably keep the cracks relatively small. Wire mesh comes in big rolls; the wires are welded at 6-inch intervals.

The strength of the concrete is an important factor to consider. Five-sack concrete, 5 sacks of cement per yard is the minimum strength to consider. Six-sack is the strongest you will need. Concrete costs increase minimally with the strength of the mix.

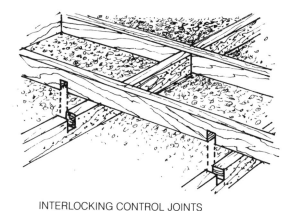

INTERLOCKING CONTROL JOINTS

Fig. 4-16. Pressure-treated lumber can be interlocked to form both retaining walls and separators and left in place to be part of the final design.

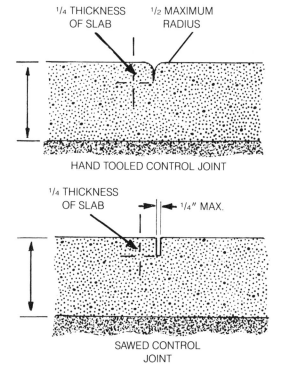

¹/₄ THICKNESS OF SLAB   ¹/₂ MAXIMUM RADIUS

HAND TOOLED CONTROL JOINT

¹/₄ THICKNESS OF SLAB   ¹/₄" MAX.

SAWED CONTROL JOINT

Fig. 4-17. A control joint helps the concrete break in an even line in the event of future ground movement or settling.

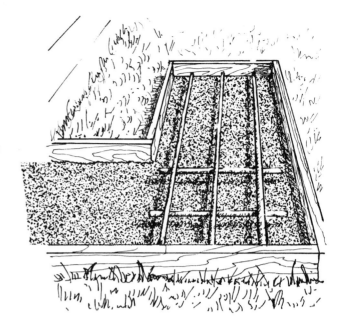

Fig. 4-18. Wire or control bars reinforce the concrete slab.

Pouring the Concrete

This is the toughest part of the job. Make certain you have rested thoroughly and have a couple of friends standing by to help. The cool ones come after the job is finished, not before. Hopefully the concrete truck can get to your patio site, if not, you will have to wheelbarrow the stuff to your site. This part of the job must be done quickly before the concrete sets up. Have several shovels nearby as you will have to toss concrete into corners and fill up valleys or topple hills of the grey stuff. Don't try for perfection at this point as the next step will level out the hills and valleys.

Screeding

Screeding is a term you won't find in your dictionary. It is a term that refers to a board that is moved back and forth in a sawing motion to draw the excess concrete off the forms (Fig. 4-19). This is usually a 2 × 4 cut the length of the patio span. The board is held on edge to minimize sag and to pull more concrete. Gradually drag the excess off, fill in the low spots with shovels full of concrete if necessary. This will give you a rough flat surface that is now ready to float.

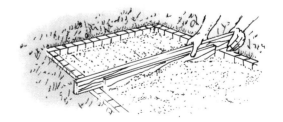

Fig. 4-19. Screeding levels and removes excess concrete.

Floating Concrete

Floating is designed to press the large particles down into the mix below and float sand and cement to the surface to make a relatively smooth surface. When you are floating the concrete, it will be too soft to stand on, even on a kneeling board. If the area is narrow enough that you can reach the center from the forming boards, a hand-held trowel can be used for this purpose. If the area is large, you will need a bull float or darby with a long handle to finish the task. A piece of plywood attached to a 2 × 4 will do the job also (Fig.

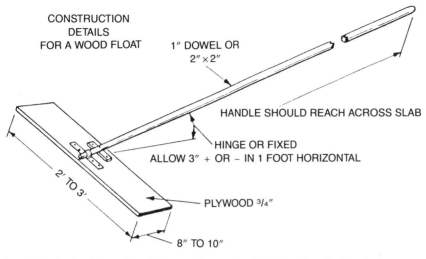

Fig. 4-20. A simple floating device can be made with a 1 × 8 and a 2 × 2.

4-20). Push and pull the float across the surface until the large particles have disappeared, and the surface is watery and smooth. If you desire a sandy surface or if this is the base for bricks or tile, floating will be enough.

Edging

Edging the concrete is the process of running a metal edging tool between the concrete and the forming boards around the outside perimeter (Fig. 4-21). This finished edge will resist cracking when the forms are removed later.

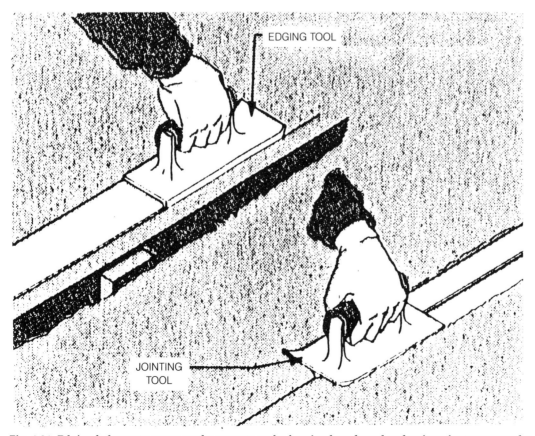

Fig. 4-21. Edging helps put a curve on the concrete at the forming boards and makes it easier to remove the boards. Jointing puts a joint in the concrete to compensate for future earth movement or settlement.

Troweling

Troweling is the process of creating a smooth surface. Troweling is done in three stages. On the first pass, the trowel is kept flat to the surface of the concrete. On the second pass, lift the leading edge of the trowel off the surface and press harder with the back edge. On the third and final pass, exaggerate step two (Fig. 4-22). Quite a smooth surface can be created in this manner.

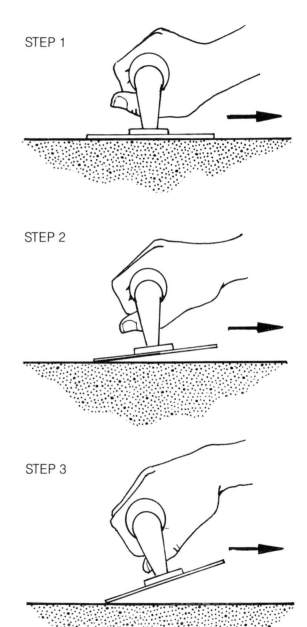

Fig. 4-22. Troweling is done in three steps.

Broom Finish

After your concrete has been floated and/or troweled, varying degrees of texture can be added with a broom. Always draw the broom toward you across the surface of the concrete (Fig. 4-23). Three factors will affect the degree of texture, the stiffness of the broom bristles, the wetness of the concrete, and the wetness of the broom.

Fig. 4-23. A broom finish textures the concrete surface and makes it easier to walk on without fear of slipping.

Grooved or Stamped Finishes

These finishes are created with metal stamping devices or grooving tools (Fig. 4-24). Commercial stamping devices are designed to make the shape of bricks, pavers, or stones in your concrete. You can make your own device from pipe or bar stock. I have seen round bricks created from the end of a 6-inch PVC pipe that was pushed into the cement. With an ordinary metal rod, you can create a lot of free hand shapes (Fig. 4-25).

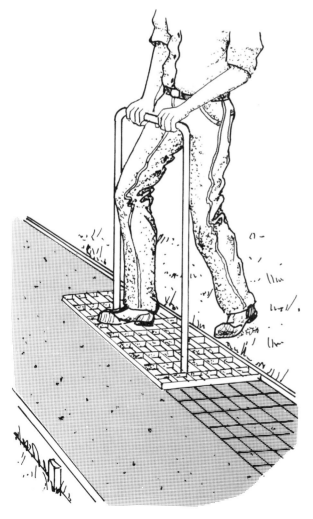

Fig. 4-24. Metal molds can be used to make shapes in the wet concrete.

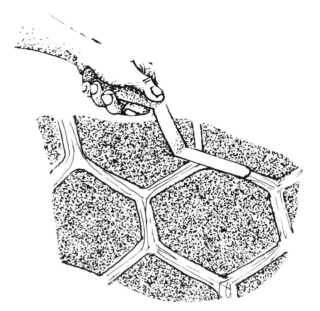

Fig. 4-25. Shapes can be carved in wet concrete with special tools.

Colored Finishes

If you want color in your concrete there are two different ways to do it. First you can have a mineral pigment added to the mix (do not exceed 10 percent of the weight). If you are going to be making more than one batch, measure the mix very carefully to maintain an even color between batches. A second method is to apply dry dye to the surface after it has been leveled and floated. Apply $2/3$ of the material on the first application and trowel as usual. Apply the remaining $1/3$ and finish troweling. Be certain to read the manufacturer's directions carefully.

Exposed Aggregate

This attractive finish can be accomplished in two ways. First, it can be made by hosing off the semiwet concrete surface to expose the stone material that was mixed into your concrete. If this is your plan, make certain the stone used in the mix is attractive such as river gravel or some other attractive stone. The second method is to sprinkle stones onto the surface of the concrete after it has been screeded. When you float the concrete, the stones will be pressed into the concrete just below the surface. In either case you will have to hose off the concrete to expose the aggregate after the concrete has set up enough so that you can do this without washing away the binding material holding the stone in place (Fig. 4-26).

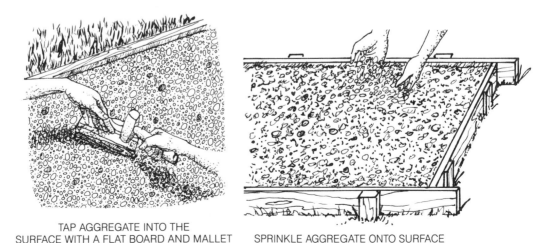

TAP AGGREGATE INTO THE
SURFACE WITH A FLAT BOARD AND MALLET   SPRINKLE AGGREGATE ONTO SURFACE

Fig. 4-26. Exposed aggregate makes a beautiful finish.

BRICK, PAVERS, AND STONE PATIO CONSTRUCTION

The method for laying bricks, pavers, and stone are all very similar. I will describe them all as a unit in this section. As previously mentioned, a good base is essential for a long patio life. I use the generic word *paver* in this discussion and description. Patio bases fall into the following categories:

Concrete. A 4- to 6-inch slab of concrete with rough surface.

Gravel or Chat. A 4- to 6-inch layer of gravel, preferably limestone, with small (fine) particles in it.

Sand. A 2-inch layer is suitable in areas that don't freeze.

Compacted Dirt. Only suitable for large flagstones.

These bases represent a descending order of stability and therefore, desirability. They also represent the descending order of costs. They are all suitable for either brick, pavers, or stone patios.

A concrete base is unified, but the other more motile mediums need to be supported by stable edging or borders to contain the fields of material inside. See the Edgings, Steps, and Walkways section on how to plan and build a successful border.

In the case of a concrete base, you might want to set the patio surface material into a bed of mortar. The bed of mortar will adhere the patio to the base and help take up some of the irregularities inherent in stone and some other pavers. Your mortar bed can be from 1/2 to 1-inch thick depending on the conditions you are working under. Work an area 10 square feet and under. Using a mason's line, a level, a rubber mallet, a wooden block, and a 1/2-inch spacer, start in one corner and work your way out from there. Tap the paving into line and level. Allow it to set up for four hours before putting the mortar between your pavers or stone with a small trowel. When the joints have been filled, strike them off with a tuckpointing tool for neatness. Use a wet burlap sack after about two hours to remove any spillage before it sets up (Fig. 4-27).

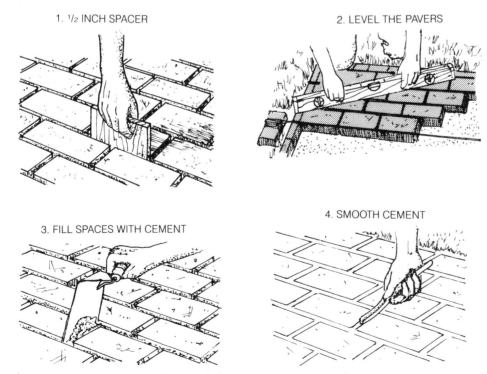

1. 1/2 INCH SPACER

2. LEVEL THE PAVERS

3. FILL SPACES WITH CEMENT

4. SMOOTH CEMENT

Fig. 4-27. Setting a patio into mortar on a concrete base.

On a gravel or sand base, you will not set your pavers into mortar. They will be laid dry and tapped or tamped into the base with a mallet and wood block. Keep some coarse trap sand to sprinkle on the gravel base to provide more give for bedding the pavers. Remember to use a 1/2-inch spacer to provide uniform joints. When your entire patio is finally in place, sweep a dry prepared sand/cement mortar mix into the joints until they are filled. Check the joints and tamp the space to ensure that they are full. Using a hose, lightly sprinkle the entire surface to soak the mortar in the joints. In about a half hour these joints can be tooled; in two hours, they can be washed down with a burlap sack to remove any excess mortar (Fig. 4-28).

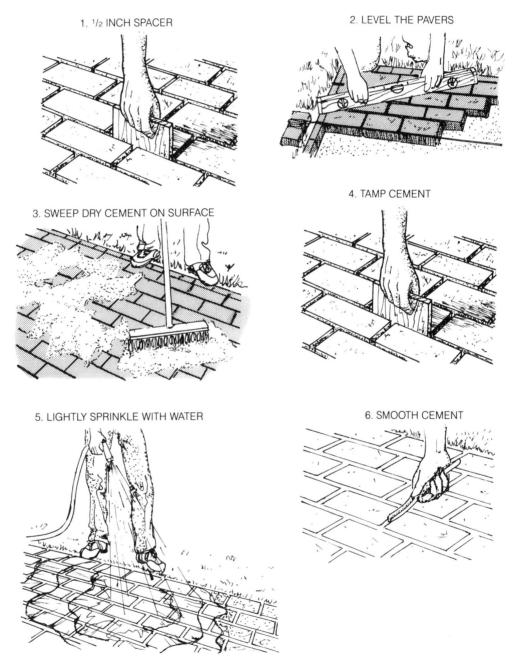

Fig. 4-28. Setting a patio into a gravel or sand base.

EDGINGS, STEPS, AND WALKWAYS

Edgings

Edgings are divided into three basic categories:

1. Light edgings to hold stones or mulch

2. Masonry-retained edgings

3. Earth-retained edgings

Light edgings can be made from wood, steel, plastic, bricks, stones, or many other materials such as the vinyl and plastic stuff they sell at home centers. Their primary purpose is to define one area of a patio or landscaping from another. For example, separating a lawn from a garden or a unique batch of plants and flowers from a patio, walkway, or yard.

Some examples of wood edgings are redwood and pressure-treated yellow pine 2 × 4s, railroad ties, landscape timbers, etc. These are normally placed to extend above the ground just enough to retain the material within them (Fig. 4-29). Metal edgings make a very precise edge that can be formed into curves. Plastic and vinyl edgings are also flexible, but like metal they require metal stakes to hold them in place. Bricks and stone can be lined up and partially buried in the ground to hold their position (Fig. 4-30). They make very attractive and durable edgings. Wood 2 × 4s can be kerfed and bent to make interesting curves and other shapes.

Fig. 4-29. Inexpensive plastic edgings can help define an area or separate one area from the other.

Fig. 4-30. This is an excellent example of wood retainers.

Masonry edgings perform the task of containing a patio or walkway of brick, stone, or pavers. Masonry edgings are made of material that matches or contrasts with the patio it defines (Fig. 4-31). A brick patio can be edged with matching bricks, contrasting bricks, or an entirely different material such as stone. These edgings are normally set in a continuous trough of concrete around the perimeter of the patio. It is a good idea to add some rebar or steel wire to the shallow footings into which you set your edgers. This embedded steel will hold the perimeter together even if the concrete cracks.

Earth retaining edgings are usually made of heavy timbers such as railroad ties, concrete, or brick walls. I will confine our discussion here to low structures because the next section covers retaining walls. A good example of an earth-retaining edging is a raised planter made from railroad ties. Put rock into the bottom for drainage and add 9 to 10 inches of good topsoil. Pressure-treated landscape timbers work well for smaller structures. Dry laid stone such as limestone (lannon stone) makes a beautiful and durable way to retain a small hillside (Fig. 4-32).

Step Construction

I will not attempt to list all the materials that steps can be constructed from. The list is big and virtually all the materials discussed this far can be worked into steps in some fashion. I am focusing here on railroad ties and concrete for steps which work well on their own or as the base for other paving materials.

Railroad-tie steps are made as a series of overlapping level platforms spiked together (Fig. 4-33). While it is possible to set ties into a hillside, corner-to-corner, this does not make a very stable construction and is difficult to walk. Railroad ties are available in two sizes, 6 × 6 and 6 × 8. Using the 6 × 6 variety as an example, cut two, three-foot pieces into the hillside. Make them level and parallel. Their measurement, outside-to-outside will be the width of your steps. Cut one tie to fit between them and another to fit across the front of all

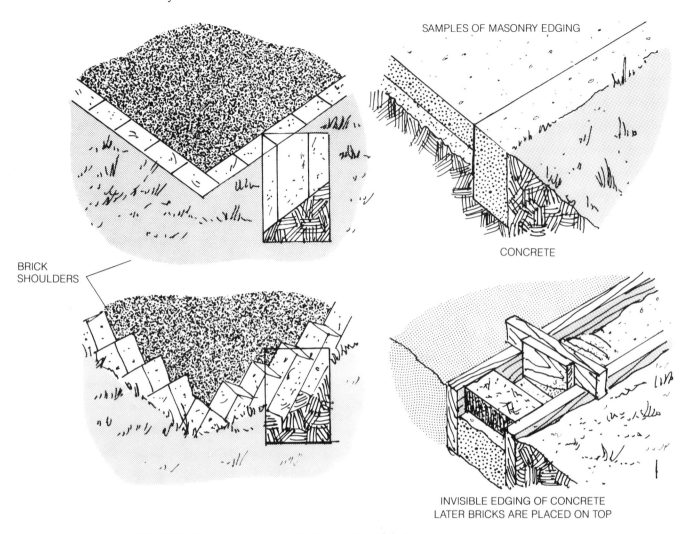

SAMPLES OF MASONRY EDGING

CONCRETE

BRICK
SHOULDERS

INVISIBLE EDGING OF CONCRETE
LATER BRICKS ARE PLACED ON TOP

Fig. 4-31. Masonry edgers provide for a variety of designs.

Fig. 4-32. These limestone edgers provide an attractive low wall and can be made from found material.

Fig. 4-33. Timbers make excellent steps as well as retainers.

three. This forms the first platform. The next platform is constructed on top of this but extends further into the hillside. Repeat the process so that the front piece overlaps the central piece by an inch or so. Spike the railroad ties together and to the ties in the level below.

Concrete steps are a bit tricky to form and pour, but with the help of these directions and diagrams you will be able to master a set of steps in no time. Visualize steps as a 4-inch concrete base onto which the step shapes are attached. This base is essential for stability and for maintaining the desired position of the steps. A pier or two at the bottom will enhance the stability of the steps in parts of the country where freeze/thaw cycles occur.

Let's assume we are making a 3-step project. The first step is to clear the area and dig to a depth of 4 to 6 inches. Cut 3/4-inch plywood in the shape of the steps you want to make. Securely brace these side boards in place with 2 × 4s on the outside of the forms. Fill in the open space with rubble (stone, brick, or old concrete pieces) to within four inches of the bottom of the riser boards (Fig. 4-34). Be certain to leave space next to the plywood forms so the concrete can fill in the open area and no rubble will show when the forms are removed. If you live in an area where the freeze/thaw is severe you might want to dig piers and fill with concrete before this step. Next, nail suitable sized boards to the front of each step, which forms the step riser. This leaves the step tread area open for pouring the concrete.

Fig. 4-34. This is a common form for pouring concrete steps.

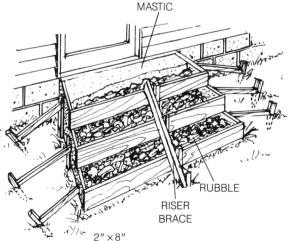

Next, oil the forms with some motor oil or other suitable product. Pour the concrete and tamp in place. The concrete must be dry enough to stay within the step shapes without overflowing. Trowel the steps to have about a $1/4$-inch drop to shed water. When the concrete has set up, (the next day) remove the forms and fill in any irregularities with topping mix while the concrete is still green. The steps must be allowed to cure slowly, especially if they were poured in hot, dry weather. To cure the concrete, cover it with wet gunny or burlap sacks. Keep this project wet for three or four days. Slow curing of concrete allows it to achieve its greatest strength.

Walkways

Walkways are the transitions from one area of the patio to another, from your patio to a backyard structure or just around the house (Fig. 4-35). They will often contain steps or ramping sections to account for slopes in your land (Fig. 4-36). Short walkways look best if they are made from the same material or match the patio appearance. Some patio treatments can be costly making long walkways too great an expense. If this is true, make your walkway from gravel or more decorative small stones, wood chips, or pole bark. Line the sides with landscaping timbers, railroad ties, or pressure-treated 2 × 4s. You can use branches from trees to also define the path although they will not last the years as other products. If you use this method I strongly suggest you spray the walkway with pesticides and other chemicals to discourage plant growth.

Fig. 4-35 and 4-36. These are excellent examples of transitions from one part of the patio to another.

Fig. 4-36.

5

Supporting and Retaining Wall Construction

IN THE LANDSCAPING OR CONSTRUCTION OF A PATIO IN A YARD THERE ARE TIMES WHEN YOU have to retain soil. That is, figure out a way to keep it from washing away or crumbling. Perhaps you live in a hilly area, and the only way to put in a patio is to remove dirt to create a flat area (Fig. 5-1). You have to retain the soil on the uphill side of the patio. Perhaps you live in a totally flat area, and you want to create terraced gardens or living areas (Fig. 5-2). What is the best way to retain the soil?

For most homeowners, the only two ways to retain soil that are practical, is either with a concrete wall or a wall built with railroad ties or treated timbers. Stone, either loose or cemented, is usable for very small walls or edgings. Brick, except when used as a veneer, or for small walls or edgings, is not practical (Fig. 5-3).

As a rule of thumb, try and keep the slope on your bank or in your yard, under 45 degrees. The higher you build your retaining wall, the gentler the slope behind it. Unfortunately this also means a greater force to retain, which in turn can eventually move or destroy the wall. It is the proper calculation of the force that must be retained that will lead the way to building to a secure and long lasting retaining wall.

CONCRETE RETAINING WALLS

Generally speaking, concrete is really not very attractive by itself. But, it does offer the easiest and fastest way to put in a strong retaining wall. Properly reinforced concrete will last over a lifetime. There are two factors to deal with in the construction of a concrete retaining wall:

1. The force to be retained

2. Elimination of water pressure buildup

Table 5-1, which shows retaining wall construction data, should be referenced when computing the size and height of your retaining wall. Figure 5-4 illustrates one method of wall construction. You have many options from which to choose depending on your site considerations and taste.

Water in the soil can build up behind the wall and add additional stress to the structure

Fig. 5-1. This retaining wall integrates steps with flower beds.

Fig. 5-2. This retaining wall holds back a slope and provides for shrubbery-planting wells.

Fig. 5-3. Bricks rarely hold up under the pressure of hillsides; concrete with retaining rods and bars does a better job.

Retaining Wall Construction Data

Exposed Wall Height (A)	Top Thickness (B)	Distance from Ground to Base (C)	Distance from Top to Base (D)	Base Depth (E)	Base Width (F)	Outside Base Extension (G)	Inside Base Extension (H)
12″	6″	4″	16″	6″	14″	3″	3″
18″	6″	6″	24″	6″	18″	3″	3″
24″	7″	8″	32″	8″	24″	4″	4″
30″	7″	10″	40″	10″	28″	4″	4″
36″	8″	12″	48″	12″	36″	6″	6″
42″	8″	14″	56″	12″	40″	6″	6″
48″	9″	16″	64″	12″	44″	6″	6″

(Fig. 5-5). Proper drainage is therefore a major consideration when constructing the wall. Proper drain holes strategically placed will resolve this problem. There are three simple steps to follow to accomplish this. First, install 2-inch pipe through the forms as they are built. These should be placed 2 to 4 inches above the ground level and should slope slightly downhill. These are called *weep holes*. Next, install a second set of weep holes at the three-foot level. If your wall is shorter, forget step two. Next fill the space behind the weep holes with large rock, 2 inches or larger. Do not use fine stone or sand as this will clog up the drain. The last step is to install a gutter at the top to carry-off the surface water.

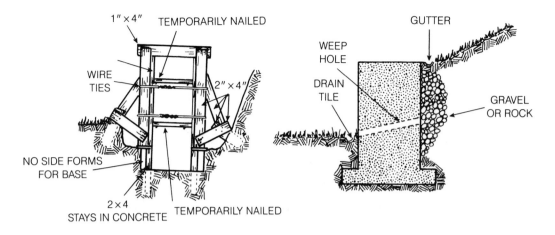

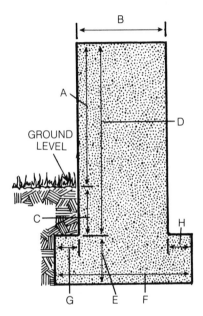

Fig. 5-4. Notice the weep/drain holes in this wall.

Fig. 5-5. This weep hole was placed too high, also a second weep hole should have been added for a wall this height.

Building the forms to retain the concrete is always the time consuming job. Proper form construction is essential if you want the wall to last. Take your time. If you do not have experience with pouring concrete, read a good book on masonry. Get some friends to help; make it into a party. Quikrete®, a manufacturer of concrete products, has a book with Don Knots on the cover that says "if I can do it, you can do it." It would be a valuable addition to your reference library.

RAILROAD TIE AND TIMBER RETAINING WALLS

Railroad ties make great retaining walls, unfortunately they don't last as long as concrete (Fig. 5-6). Generally speaking if you plan to live in your house into your golden retirement years, you are better off buying new ties than used ones. Used ties, no matter what shape they are in will not last as long as new ties or timbers.

Fig. 5-6. Used railroad ties make attractive retaining walls and steps.

Railroad ties are available in most areas in two sizes, 6 × 6 and 6 × 8. They are usually available in 8-foot lengths, but can be found in 12-foot and 16-foot lengths as well. Timbers, sold at most homecenters and nurseries come in 6-inch × 6-inch × 8-foot square and 3½-inch thick rounded variations. We suggest you get Wolmanized Extra™ water-resistant treated timbers. Other forms of pressure-treated wood won't last as long.

The term *dead men* is used in wood and railroad tie wall construction. This does not refer to the literal sense of the word. *Dead men* timbers or ties are installed at right angles to the face of the wall, into the ground, behind the wall, into the bank. Normally dead men are 4 feet to 8 feet long depending on the force of the hill above and behind the wall. The idea behind the use of dead men is that it uses the weight of the bank or hill, to keep the wall or facing ties or timbers in place (Fig. 5-7).

Timbers and ties must be securely nailed to one another. Use 10-inch spikes for this purpose. Toenail the ties and timber ends to the dead men using 30-penny nails.

Fig. 5-7. Deadmen ties make an interesting wall.

Since water is the main culprit in the destruction of wood, make certain the ties and timbers are properly treated products. Pressure-treated lumber has been tested to last up to 30 years or more in the ground. Untreated timbers might not even last two or three years in some locations (Figs. 5-8, 5-9).

Fig. 5-8. These deadmen ties were used to make terraced gardens.

Fig. 5-9. This cleverly designed fence uses deadmen ties to section-off trees.

Fig. 5-10. This is an example of bricks used as a veneer with concrete for a retaining wall.

BRICK AND STONE WALL CONSTRUCTION

The only successful application of bricks in retaining wall construction is as a veneer to a concrete wall. Brick walls, which are porous and built up of small units mortared together, often fall victim to the ravages of freezing and thawing and eventually fall over. Very low brick walls will be most successful in warm climates. Brick walls are ideal when used as dividers or as screens provided they have the proper footing (Fig. 5-10).

Stone such as limestone, which is generally a fairly flat stone, can be used to retain soil or as a veneer to a concrete wall. Like bricks, in time, stone will also fall over (Fig. 5-11). The best application of stone is for low ridges or for retaining soil in a planting or shrubbery application (Figs. 5-12, 5-13). The one benefit of stone is that it is as close as the nearest highway construction site or creek bed.

Fig. 5-11. This retaining wall from found stone is not sloped properly and is too high; it will not last.

Fig. 5-12. Notice the slope or tilt of this stone retaining wall. It is designed to resist the earth movement.

Fig. 5-13. This stone retaining wall with mortar makes the best stone or brick retainer.

6

Overhead Covers, Shading, and Screens

YOU CAN'T ENJOY OUTDOOR LIVING ON YOUR DECK WHEN THE WIND IS BLOWING 90 MILES an hour, when it is raining, or when the sun is beating down so hot that you can fry an egg on the patio (Fig. 6-1). A roof or sun shade can provide you and your family the protection you need to enjoy your deck and patio, not only all through the day but over an extended period of the year as well. Being outdoors sitting under protection and being able to enjoy a summer storm can be a thrilling experience.

There are a wide variety of materials that can be used for deck and patio covering, shading, and screening. They can be glass, bamboo, plastic, metal, wood, reed, fencing, and others. The effect you want to achieve will be the determining factor in your selection of materials (Fig. 6-2).

LOAD-BEARING ROOFS

Our first discussion will include roofs that exclude rain and sun and can support snow weight. These roofs are constructed much like the roof over your house (Fig. 6-3). They are sloped or semiflat using shingles, hot tar, or rubber membrane. All the necessary structural factors that go into building a deck must be considered here. The rafters, beams sheathing, and roofing materials are quite heavy by themselves, but in most locales the additional burden of snow load must be taken into account. Be certain to consult a local engineer, familiar with your area of the country, to avoid the hazards inherent in constructing a structure too lightly. Another satisfactory roof in this category is corrugated sheet metal, the proverbial "tin roof." Many other opaque, water resistant materials such as exterior plywood or tempered masonite will also work (Fig. 6-4).

SUN ROOFS

The next category of roofs exclude precipitation, but allow the sun to shine through. A glass or clear dome roof will allow the sun to shine through but keep out the rain. The problem is it will also give a greenhouse effect in direct sun unless the rays are broken by some kind of partial shading. Another way to achieve a similar effect is with translucent roofing material (Fig. 6-5). The most common material for this purpose is plastic or fiberglass panels. While corrugated or rippled fiberglass panels are similar in appearance to the sheet

Fig. 6-1. A basic frame such as this can support lattice, canvas, or any number of screen or shade material.

Fig. 6-2. This lattice screen covers a patio separating the garage and house.

Fig. 6-3. This is one example of a partial cover over a deck.

Fig. 6-4. Inexpensive plastic covers provide shelter over this patio.

Fig. 6-5. Screen provides the shading in this cover.

metal panels and are installed in the same fashion, they offer the advantage of filtered light transmission. Plastic roofing can be very strong material such as Lexan plastic that football helmets are made out of. However, they can also be quite temporary materials such as plastic sheeting found at low cost at most hardware stores. This material will not hold up through a long hot summer, a winter, or a hail storm.

CANVAS ROOFS

Canvas, depending on how it is installed, makes a very attractive rainproof roof. Many canvas awnings today are stretched over a light metal pipe frame. Such an application can be beyond the scope of most do-it-yourselfers, but it can be a very attractive way to add a splash of color to your finished project (Fig. 6-6). Canvas can be laced into openings for a

Fig. 6-6. This is an example of a simple canvas cover in a deck corner.

wind break or privacy screen quite successfully. You will need a grommet setting tool, a hole punch, and grommet/rivets that snap together. You will also have to be very friendly with someone who has a very sturdy sewing machine, or you can hire an upholsterer to do the sewing for you. Commercial installations of canvas are not cheap, and this is not the least expensive way to provide a roof.

WOOD-SLAT ROOFS

The next category of roofing is not rainproof and has a narrow life expectancy if not properly maintained and cleaned. The life of sun shades is in direct proportion to how much sun or shade it deals with or how many leaves it withstands. Both of these last two conditions slow drying time after a rain and can promote the growth of mold or fungus. These attack wood and woodlike products and also hasten the demise of synthetic products as well.

One shade solution using wood involves the installation of spaced boards (Fig. 6-7). The choice of board size and spacing is very broad (Fig. 6-8). A few attractive combinations are:

Board size	Spacing	Support distance
1×4	1¹/₂" to 2"	36"
2×2	1¹/₂"	36"
2×4 on edge	1¹/₂" to 2"	72"
2×6 on edge	2" to 4"	96"

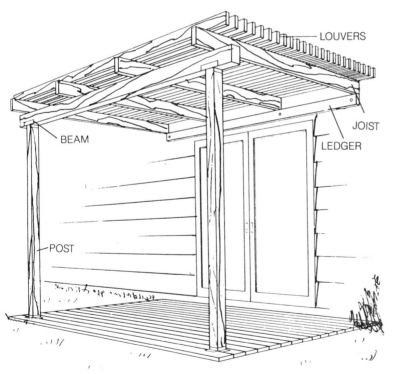

Fig. 6-7 and 6-8. These are examples of louver covers.

Other solutions using wood include:

- split-fence boards (more rustic) (Figs. 6-9, 6-10)
- wood and wire fencing
- lattice (Fig. 6-11)
- slat blinds
- wooden louvers (Fig. 6-12)
- egg crate design boards
- match-stick bamboo
- reed matting

Fig. 6-9. Another example of wood slats for cover.

Fig. 6-10. A split fence using wood boards.

Fig. 6-11. Lattice screening and shading.

LOUVERS

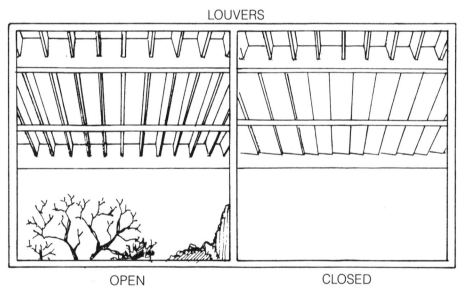

OPEN   CLOSED

Fig. 6-12. This is an example of moveable louvers that can be adjusted to fit the angle of the sun and the time of day.

SCREENS

Other shade producing materials include shade-screen which is especially designed for the landscaping industry. This material is available in various graded densities.

Insect Screening

This material is an absolute must, especially if you have to fight mosquitoes in your area. Those little creatures can turn your deck into a torment chamber very quickly.

Screening is available in grey aluminum, plastic, brass, bright aluminum, and fiberglass. If you decide to screen your deck, don't forget to screen the open areas around the supporting piers and posts, or the little buggers will get in from below.

7

Walls, Fences, and Dividers

THERE ARE MANY ADVANTAGES TO PROVIDING YOUR DECK OR PATIO PROJECT WITH DIVIDERS, such as for the formation of intimate sections for entertaining. Perhaps you need a wall on one side for wind and sun protection or a wood fence that divides your patio and provides privacy and security. For purpose of this discussion, I am going to take editorial liberty to loosely define walls as structures of brick, stone, or concrete. Fences being structures primarily of wood or metal (Figs. 7-1A, 7-1B), and dividers as structures whose main function is appearance. These divisions are admittedly quite arbitrary but will help in organizing our discussion of these subjects.

Fig. 7-1A and 7-1B. These pressure-treated pickets and basket weave are two examples of the use of wood for fencing and dividers.

WALLS

We have discussed how to build retaining walls. Their main function was to hold back the ground on one side of the wall. The walls, we will discuss here, are for privacy, safety/security, weather protection, and so forth. The construction basics, however, are the same for both kinds of walls, namely a solid foundation below the frost/freezing level. Masonry and stone can be expected to last a lifetime if their mortar bonds are not broken by the ravages of weather.

Some photographs are provided in this section for various wall types to give you some thoughts or ideas for your own situation.

Walls for privacy are designed to keep the world from seeing you or vice versa. Perhaps you have a swimming pool that local laws consider an attractive nuisance. Local ordinances will specify wall heights. The problem is how to hide it from the general public and provide security and beauty at the same time (Figs. 7-2, 7-3). A masonry wall can be made to blend in with the decor or natural setting.

If you need a wind break or something to hide the afternoon sun, a tall wall is the perfect answer (Fig. 7-4). The types of walls you can build are varied. You can have a straight masonry wall, a serpentine, or intermittent wall. A serpentine wall is especially strong because of its sinuous shape. Not all walls have to be made from solid materials (Fig. 7-5). There are a number of hollow products such as concrete block, clay, and fired clay elements. Interesting walls can be made by embedding glass blocks or wine bottles into the primary mortar. Bricks can be laid to leave openings in the wall. All of these techniques add a visual excitement to a medium that can be bland. Consider too the idea of using individual wall elements separated by space (Fig. 7-6). These can be set at an angle or at alternating angles like herringbone. The possibilities are only limited by your imagination (Fig. 7-7).

Fig. 7-2 and 7-3. These above-ground and inground swimming pools are surrounded by wood fencing that provides security and privacy.

Fig. 7-4. This pool is protected by a brick fence.

Fig. 7-5. This metal fence says first class.

Fig. 7-6. This combination of wood and brick provides a territorial boundary and yet does not shut out the view.

Fig. 7-7. This stone wall makes an elegant fence.

FENCES

Fences can perform many of the functions of walls, but are easier to install and a lot less expensive. The main drawback is that walls will generally outlast fences. The fence construction methods that will be addressed here are those for wood and metal fences.

Fences are typically constructed by first setting line and corner posts at regular intervals; eight-foot spacing seems to be the most acceptable (Fig. 7-8). Also, it is better for esthetic reasons to keep the spacing uniform, but eight feet or less should be adhered to. The second element of a fence is the rails that are usually installed horizontally. The third element is pickets, usually installed vertically. Fence designs are so varied that it is impossible to cover every possibility, but many fences have these elements in common.

Fig. 7-8. Fence posts can be set in concrete or supported by wood cross members in the ground. This can only be effectively done with pressure-treated lumber.

Line and corner posts are usually set into the ground. Select a timber that is at least a 4 × 4″ or thicker and two feet or more longer than the height intended to show above the ground. The additional length is to be buried in the ground for support. The hole is usually dug with a post-hole digger, a special kind of shovel designed for this purpose. The hole is backfilled with the original dirt from the hole or preferably concrete. Sacks of premix are the best for this project and usually provide more than enough mix for one post hole. Regardless of the method of backfill, make certain the post is straight and plumb. Use a level for this purpose.

These posts will be in constant contact with the ground. It is very important that you choose posts that are durable materials suitable for damp locations. Pressure-treated lumber is the most highly recommended wood product of choice. Based upon tests, it can last 25 years or longer in the ground. Redwood would be the second best, and a poor third, western red cedar. Other normally available woods are really not suitable. Many farmers in my area of the Ozarks have used red cedar logs over the years for fence posts, but even this product is not suited for any kind of permanent fence construction.

Some fences add only the rail elements to the posts such as the two-rail fence or paddled-rail fence. A decorative ranch or corral fence is similar but employs the use of diagonal elements as well. Another fence type that is very attractive is a basket weave design (Fig. 7-9).

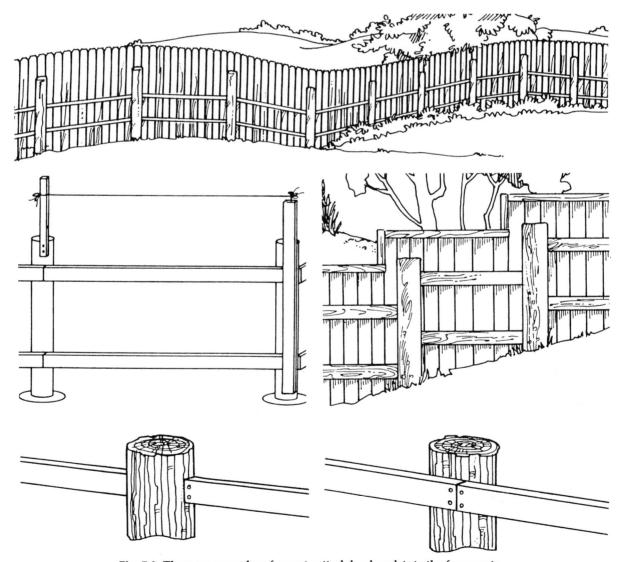

Fig. 7-9. These are examples of ways to attach lumber slats to the fence posts.

If you want to add pickets to your fence design, the rails are used to support them. As a rule of thumb, you will need one rail for each two feet of fence height. For example, four-foot height—2 rails, six-foot height—3 rails, etc. The rails are normally placed at 6 inches to 1 foot from the top and bottom of the post with other rails evenly spaced in between. Some picket type fences are stockade, grape stake, board-on-board, spaced picket (Fig. 7-10), shadow box, split bamboo, or lattice.

Fig. 7-10. One example of a spaced-picket fence.

Some special fences are panel and louver types. A *panel fence* uses a solid thin element such as canvas or plywood in a pleasing pattern to fill in for privacy between the posts and rails. A *louver fence* uses boards installed at a constant angle, one after another. The louvers can be installed either vertical or horizontal, fixed or moveable.

Methods for putting fences together fall into the categories of nails, screws, bolts, and structural metal fasteners and wood joints. All metal fasteners should be either hot-dipped galvanized or a noncorroding metal such as brass or aluminum. Dacrotized screws are another form of coated products but hold up better than galvanized products. Typically common nails are used to toenail fence rails to posts, and casing or finishing nails are used to attach the pickets. A metal hanger similar to a joist hanger, but sized for 2 × 4s makes a very strong bond between the post and the rail. Because of the cost, bolts and lag screws are reserved for attaching hardware such as gate hinges and latches where added strength is needed. Fences are fairly static and do not need the same structural considerations as a load bearing project such as a deck.

The kinds of joints employed in fence construction include lap, butt, mortised, rabbeted post, or grooved post.

Gates for fences have to be constructed in a much sturdier way than the fence (Figs. 7-11, 7-12). It has to hold up to a lot of movement and banging and its occasional use as a swing for children. Braces are needed to crossbar the gate, which creates a diagonal cross that starts on the high side of one side of the gate and ends at the low side of the other side where the hinge will be attached. This transfers the load from the free side of the fence to the hinge side for strength.

Fig. 7-11. This is a board-on-board fence.

Fig. 7-12. This gate is a combination of slat and lattice.

Hinges come in three types for gate use: strap, tee, and butt. A number of different latches are available plus you can make your own from wood. Make certain the metal is coated to prevent rust.

Metal fences also fit into this category, although they are generally not as attractive when mixed with your new patio or deck. Check with local suppliers for directions and the special tools you might need for installation.

You can also mix wood and wrought iron and brick and other materials to create very attractive fences.

DIVIDERS

Dividers, as the name implies, are used within a deck or patio area to add visual interest or to define spaces within a larger area (Figs. 7-13, 7-14). Some examples of this would be an attractive or decorative low fence, a group of planters, a bench, a fountain, or a combination planter-bench that creates the right visual look for your area.

Fig. 7-13. This wood divider provides some privacy on this low-level deck.

Fig. 7-14. This fence is designed to keep in cattle and livestock and is fairly heavy-duty construction.

8

Deck and Patio Furnishings and Cooking

THE PROJECT'S DONE. IT STANDS IN FRONT OF YOU WITH NOTHING BUT BARE DECK AND PATIO surface face and adornments. What's next? Furnishing your deck or patio, can be as easy as going to your local home center or outdoor shop and buying some yard furniture and a Weber kettle for barbeques. But that really doesn't require much imagination, and it will put a big dent in your pocketbook. What's more, when you are through, you will have furnishings just like the people next door. You can put some real class on your deck or patio, and put a lot of savings in your pocket if you make your own backyard furnishings.

In this section we provide you with some ideas and design concepts you can adapt for your own situation. From a functional barbeque and planter seater to 2 – × – 4 tables, chairs, and chaise lounges to planters, swings, and birdfeeders. Since we are limited to the space allowed in this book, writing detailed instructions to make all of these projects is prohibitive. You can get more detailed information by writing to the address in the front of this book for a list of detailed plans that are available to make these projects.

DECK AND PATIO COOKING

Hhhhot dog! Now that you have created your own special space for relaxing and partying, can't you almost smell the barbeque cooking? There is nothing more inviting than the smell of a charcoal fire and the aroma from the hickory or mesquite chips and, of course, the meat and vegetables.

This design for a barbeque makes the project a very versatile item. After the fire has died down you have both a planter and a conversation bench that also can serve as a divider (Fig. 8-1). Of course if you put this on a deck, make certain you have someone properly engineer the support below.

The size of this project is approximately 8 feet long and 12 courses of bricks high. This computes to roughly 36 inches to 48 inches depending on the amount of mortar and size of brick you use.

Choosing the right bricks is critical when doing any outdoor project like this. Type I bricks are suitable for general use especially where there is heavy frost and cold weather. Make certain the bricks you buy are uniform. Two bricks struck together should produce a ringing sound like a ceramic bell; this indicates they are of good quality. Use heat-resistant

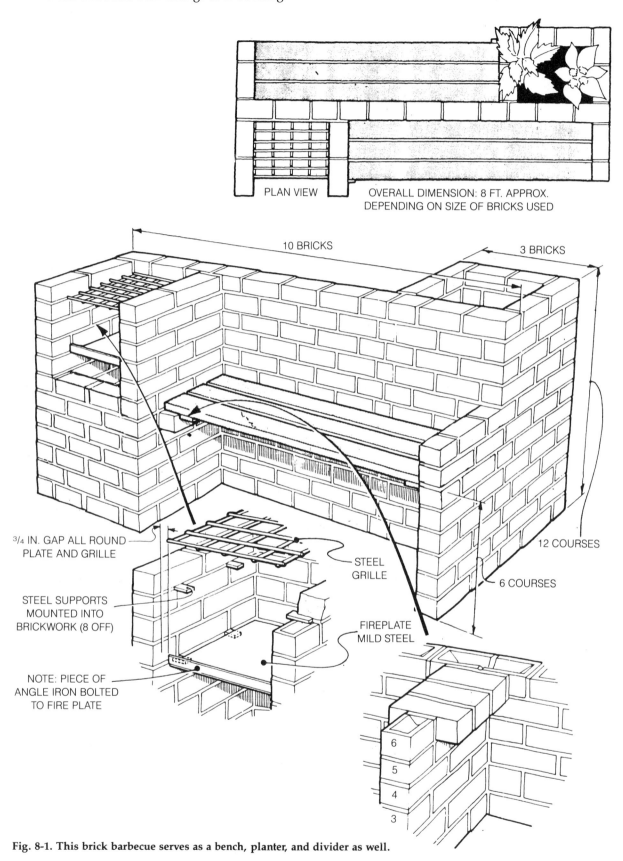

PLAN VIEW

OVERALL DIMENSION: 8 FT. APPROX.
DEPENDING ON SIZE OF BRICKS USED

10 BRICKS

3 BRICKS

³/₄ IN. GAP ALL ROUND
PLATE AND GRILLE

STEEL SUPPORTS
MOUNTED INTO
BRICKWORK (8 OFF)

NOTE: PIECE OF
ANGLE IRON BOLTED
TO FIRE PLATE

STEEL
GRILLE

FIREPLATE
MILD STEEL

12 COURSES

6 COURSES

6
5
4
3

Fig. 8-1. This brick barbecue serves as a bench, planter, and divider as well.

firebricks to form the barbeque box, otherwise you will have to redo the project after your first barbeque.

Use 2-foot redwood for the seating. For a really sharp appearance use a good grade of pressure-treated, radius-bias 1-inch decking material.

YARD STRUCTURES

A natural addition to any patio or deck is a gazebo or as the dictionary describes it, a summer house. These structures can be screened to protect you from the insects and yet let the natural breezes flow through (Fig. 8-2).

Fig. 8-2. These are several design options for a backyard gazebo or screened-in summer house.

Perhaps you need a pool cabanna for changing swim suits. This privy design can serve that function and also be a conversation piece (Fig. 8-3). It also can be used to store deck or patio necessities such as torch lights or cushions or even the lawnmower. I chose this design because it reminds me of one that we had when I was a kid. I remember reading the Sears and Roebuck catalogs and dreading the winter months when you got down to the slick pages.

Fig. 8-3. This privy design will make a great poolside dressing room or for the storage of garden tools as well.

We built this bird feeder to complement the deck project. This and the others are but a few of the kinds of accents that you can add to your yard, plus the birds love the handouts (Figs. 8-4A, 8-4B).

Fig. 8-4A and 8-4B. Don't forget the birds need a dining area in the backyard too.

Fig. 8-4B.

PATIO, DECK AND YARD FURNITURE

We built all of the furniture for the deck shown on the cover of this book from Wolmanized water-resistant pressure-treated lumber. With luck, these projects should be around for a long time. However, we suggest you use Thompson water seal or another good grade of stain and sealant to ensure the long lasting beauty of your projects. Most of these projects can use standard patio furniture replacement cushions that are available at most discount stores.

The rocking sling chair requires approximately 18- × -74-inch canvas. The sling is a very easy thing to make on a sewing machine, or you can have it made at any upholstery shop. We used 1-inch pressure-treated lumber for the supports (Fig. 8-5).

PVC pipe furniture, as shown, is perhaps the easiest of all the projects to make. The only tools you will need are a hacksaw, tape, measure, and drill (Fig. 8-6).

Benches and tables with the heart designs can be made from 1-inch radius-bias decking lumber scraps that are left over from the deck project. You might say they will be free furniture.

A planter bench can be made from 2- × -4 material with standard chair cushions. The plants make a natural addition, and the bench creates an interesting conversation nook in a corner of the deck.

A lattice-covered box with a cushion on top can be a storage box for deck items when they aren't needed.

We added a swinging dinosaur to the bottom of the deck for that special grandchild to use (Fig. 8-7).

Fig. 8-5. A portable rocking sling chair like this looks great on the deck or patio and is the world's most comfortable chair.

Fig. 8-6. PVC pipe furniture is simple to make and inexpensive.

Fig. 8-7. This dinosaur swing is sure to please that little one.

Nothing beats the tranquility of swinging on a yard swing (Fig. 8-8). We added this to the bottom of the deck so Grandma could swing with her grandchild.

The picnic tables in Figs. 8-9 and 8-10 were made from 2-×-6 material with surfaces made from 1-inch radius-bias decking scraps. The bases or supports were made with 4-×-4 material scraps. The umbrella can be purchased at any discount center such as K-mart or Walmart.

Fig. 8-8. The old backyard swing is always a favorite.

Fig. 8-9. This picnic table seats eight.

Fig. 8-10. This picnic table was built from left-over deck material.

The chaise lounge, chair, and table were made with scrap lattice, 1-inch and 2- × -4 lumber (Fig. 8-11). The back to the lounge folds flat for those sun worshipers in your family. The front of the chair raises up so you can rest your legs.

Fig. 8-11. This lattice lounge chair and chaise make a great addition to any backyard.

This lattice-covered bench is what I call a Sweetheart Gazebo Bench. It is fairly large, will sit 3 or more people, and is long enough to take a nap in. It was made from scrap lattice and 2- × -4 material.

What deck or patio project would be complete without an old-time glider? We used 2 × 4s and 1-inch lumber for the one in Fig. 8-12.

The patio chopping-block cart, in Fig. 8-13, has a solid 2- × -4 top. We cut the wheels from scrap 2- × -8 material. The cutting-board inset was made from hardwood strips. The storage bin was made from scrap plywood.

Fig. 8-12. This glider is perfect for relaxation at the end of the day.

Fig. 8-13. This combination is hard to beat.

Fig. 8-14. This is called the sweetheart gazebo bench.

We looked at all these projects as basically being free since they were all made from left-over materials. For a catalog of plans to build these & other projects, write to the author. P.O. Box 40, Ureka, Missouri, 63025. These are but a few of the kinds of projects you can add to your backyard, patio, and deck.

PROTECTING YOUR PATIO AND DECK

It is usually at this point that I recommend to people to go get their camera and take a color photograph of their newly completed deck or patio project. This is to remind them of what the project looked like when it was brand new. Two months from now it won't look that way unless they do something to protect the project now!

The phrase "newly completed" is important here. Whatever you do to protect your deck or patio is most effective if applied within a week of completion of your project.

Letting time slip by "because it doesn't look bad yet" can allow problems to occur. These problems come in the form of grease, dust, dirt, mildew, and dead wood fibers, all of which prevent proper penetration and adhesion of the protective chemicals.

Brick and stone patios as well as those made of concrete can all develop hairline cracks over time. A timely application of Thompson's Water Seal or similar acrylic or silicone sealers designed for masonry surfaces will bridge those cracks and keep water from penetrating. If the water is kept out, the freezing weather cannot do its seasonal damage. Allow a month of curing of concrete and two weeks for curing of mortar prior to applying these sealers. If you plan to stain the project, this must be done before the project is sealed.

Decks can be sealed, stained, and painted. If the deck has weathered and turned grey before you got around to finishing it, all is not lost. A prewash can be used to restore the original color.

If you want to color your deck, I recommend that you use a semitransparent or solid wood stain such as Olympic Deck Stain. It contains a special waterproofing agent in addition to stain in its formulation. A semitransparent stain lets the grain show through. In some cases you might want to achieve an overall solid color and hide the wood grain, in which case a solid stain is recommended. This stain has the same properties as the semitransparent stain that penetrates the wood fibers and therefore bonds tightly to the wood. Wood stains are available in oil-based and latex or acrylic (water) types. The water-based stains are easiest to clean up, but the oil-based products penetrate and adhere better.

Do not use exterior-grade acrylic paint on a deck project. It will simply not last and in short time will be flaking and chipping from the abuse of routine traffic.

Before applying stains on your deck project, go over the surface with a sander to remove pencil marks and lumber grade stamps. Remove any spots, other stains or any other offending agents. If your deck has weathered grey, a prewash such as Olympic Fresh Deck will remove this condition.

You can apply sealers with rollers, brushes, or sprays. Stains, especially semitransparent stains require special attention and are a bit more tricky to apply.

Stains are now available for concrete as well as wood. The stain must be applied before the sealer is applied.

Staining and sealing your deck and patio project is an investment that pays dividends. Simply look at the photo of the deck or patio when it was new, that will tell you that you made the right decision when you finished the project properly.

9

Lighting Your Deck and Patio

ONE OF THE MOST ATTRACTIVE AND HELPFUL ADDITIONS THAT CAN BE MADE TO ANY DECK OR patio project is outdoor lighting. You will undoubtedly wish to use your facility at night as well as during the day. Even when you are not out on the deck or on the patio, you can enjoy the relaxation it provides by having it dramatically lit. This also adds not only to your home's value, but it also affords an element of security.

LOW-VOLTAGE LIGHTING SYSTEMS

Unfortunately in today's world of high energy costs, lighting your project can get expensive. Several 75-watt light bulbs kept burning all night can add up to a healthy utility bill at month end. To combat this problem, manufacturers of light fixtures have developed new low-voltage systems that can give you better lighting with better distribution of light for a lot less money.

The low-voltage lighting systems are as easy and as safe to install as putting a little toy electric train under your Christmas tree. They are based upon the same low-voltage concept since both require a transformer. Intermatic Inc. is one of the larger manufacturers of this new product and provided the Malibu light fixtures that were used on one of the decks shown in this book.

With 120-volt systems, you must be very careful about placement of wires. They must be concealed in conduit pipe and carefully protected from the elements, especially water. A short circuit can blow the fuses and circuit breakers and cause fires. Not so with the low-voltage systems. But, other factors come into play that can cause problems.

Low-voltage systems must be on-balanced systems. That is just in the case of the toy train, if you put two or more trains operating onto the same track without adjusting the output of the transformer, each will go slower because of the drain of the transformer. Putting too many or too few lights on one transformer of a fixed output can cause the lights to burn out quickly or last a long time. It is all a balance of volts, amperes, and watts (Table 9-1).

Watts are the unit of measure that tells how much electricity is being used. The number of lights and the size and length of the wire used in a system determines the total watts of the system. You must match the transformer with the proper output in watts to the system (Table 9-2). You do not want to exceed the capacity of the transformer nor go below at least half of its output capacity. Fortunately these light systems all come in prepackaged kits so the job is rather simple.

The power packs or transformers are the heart of these light systems (Fig. 9-1). They

Table 9-1. This Table Shows the Life Expectancy of a Bulb in a Low-voltage Lighting System.

Voltage At Lamp	Life Expectancy of Lamp	Light Output (%)
12.6	2/3 Nominal Lamplife	125
12.0	3/4 Nominal Lamplife	110
11.8	Nominal Lamplife	100
11.5	1 1/2 Times Nominal Lamplife	90
11.0	3 Times Nominal Lamplife	80
10.5	5 Times Nominal Lamplife	70
10.0	8 Times Nominal Lamplife	60

Transformer Selection Chart

Total Nominal Wattage Transformer	150W 16 ga. cable		200W 14 ga. cable		250W 12 ga. cable	
	max. watts	max. length	max. watts	max. length	max. watts	max. length
60 watts	60	100	60	125	60	150
88 watts	88	100	88	125	88	150
121 watts	121	100	121	125	121	150
196 watts	150	100	150	125	196	150
224 watts	150	100	200	125	250	150
330 watts	150	100	200	150	250	200

Fig. 9-1. A small transformer is the heart of a low-voltage system.

reduce the 120 volts of your household outlet to a safe 12 volts. They are available with photoelectric cells for dusk to dawn operation. Others have an interval-time setting to turn the lights off or built-in clocks or timers to turn the lights on and off at a time you want.

A low-voltage cable distributes the power to the lights (Fig. 9-2). In order to keep the light volume equal you must use the right size of cable. As a rule of thumb 16-gauge cable is recommended for runs up to 100 feet, 14-gauge up to 150 feet, and 12-gauge for runs up to 200 feet. Another way to ensure a proper balance is to divide the cable into shorter multiple runs (Table 9-3).

Fig. 9-2. Placement of low-voltage fixtures along walkways makes the steps and sidewalk a lot safer at night.

Cable Selection Chart

	0	50	100	150	200 (feet)
16 gauge (150W)					
14 gauge (200W)					
12 gauge (250W)					

CHOOSING THE LIGHT FIXTURES

There are a wide variety of lighting fixtures that are available, or you can make your own. Each has a specific function and are placed in your yard to accomplish a certain desired effect.

Entrance Lights

These lights emit a broad downward glow that are ideal for lighting the walkway or steps and entrance to your home (Fig. 9-3).

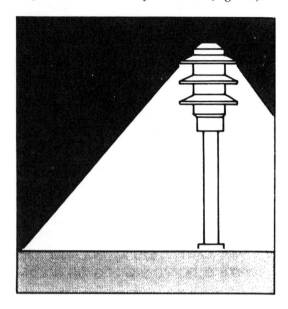

Fig. 9-3. Entrance light.

Mushroom Lights

These lights come in a variety of sizes and are used to highlight areas of low-foliage, borders, walkways, paths, and decorative ground cover (Fig. 9-4).

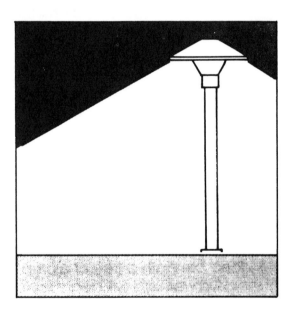

Fig. 9-4. Mushroom light.

Tier Lights

These are much like mushroom lights but also cast accents of light to flower beds and patio borders (Fig. 9-5).

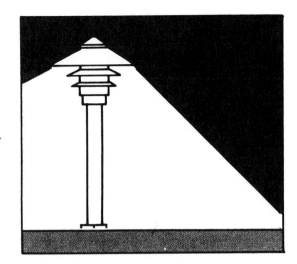

Fig. 9-5. Shaded tier light.

Well Lights

Well lights are buried into the ground and cast light upward (Fig. 9-6). They are ideal for highlighting trees and shrubs and any special area of your deck or patio.

Fig. 9-6. Well light.

Globe Lights

These lights are ideal for general diffused yard illumination (Fig. 9-7). Used around hot tubs, swimming pools, or special places in your yard that you want lots of light.

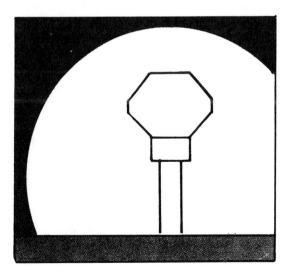

Fig. 9-7. Globe light.

Floodlights

Floodlights emit a focused ray of light much like automobile headlights (Fig. 9-8). They are great for backlighting your house or an area such as along a fence. They come with a high-intensity halogen lamp that emits whiter and brighter light than a conventional floodlight lamp. They also can be fitted with colored lenses that can give a specific effect.

Fig. 9-8. Floodlight.

Deck Lights

These are plastic and wood combinations that are designed to blend with the wooden forms of your deck (Fig. 9-9). They can be mounted underneath the banisters or railings or put on the posts.

Fig. 9-9. This fixture integrates wood and plastic into the wood atmosphere of this deck railing.

Some of the combinations of light fixture types your home could benefit from are shown in Fig. 9-10. This will provide you with ideas of the specific effects possible with all of these light fixtures.

PRODUCTS USED:
MUSHROOM LIGHTS
FLOODLIGHTS

PRODUCTS USED:
TIER LIGHTS
MUSHROOM LIGHTS
FLOODLIGHTS

PRODUCTS USED:
FLOODLIGHTS WITH COLORED LENSES
TIER LIGHTS

PRODUCTS USED:
MUSHROOM LIGHTS
FLOODLIGHTS
TIER LIGHTS

Fig. 9-10. Some combinations of light fixtures.

PRODUCTS USED:
TIER LIGHTS
WELL LIGHTS
MUSHROOM LIGHTS
ENTRANCE LIGHT

You can do your own planning for outdoor lighting by first making a layout of your yard, patio, and deck. We have provided an outdoor lighting plan in Fig. 9-11 to give you an idea of how the lighting layout can be done.

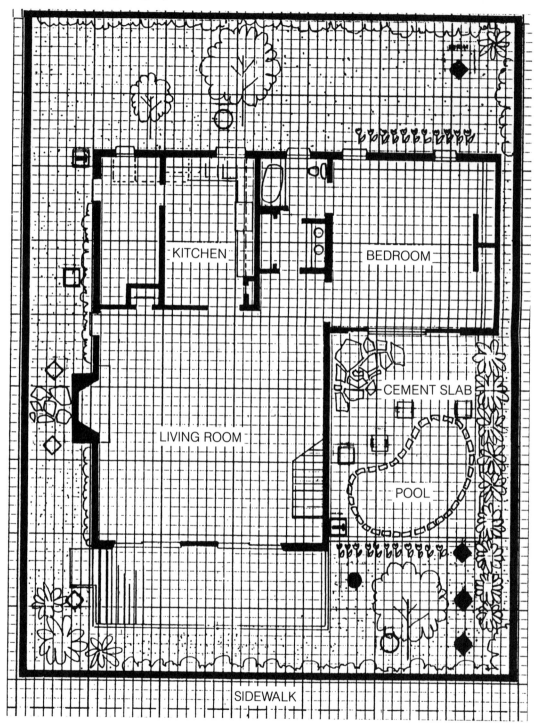

Fig. 9-11. Design for your outdoor lighting plan.

For the deck we built for this book, we used tier lighting for the entrance way, pathways, and bottoms of the steps (Fig. 9-12). Deck lights were mounted on the deck banisters and posts. We also used strip lighting for the steps. Strip lighting is also based upon the low-voltage concept. These come in convenient lengths and can also be mounted quite easily.

Fig. 9-12. These tier lights placed at the bottom of the steps will provide safety at night.

You can obtain a booklet at most home centers called, *Light Up Your Life*. It is provided by Intermatic Inc., Spring Grove, Illinois 60081 and it contains over 40 pages of lighting examples along with instructions and answers to most of your questions about this innovative lighting product. It would be a handy addition to your home-improvement library.

Index

Other Bestsellers of Related Interest

INCREASE ITS WORTH: 101 Ways To Maximize The Value of Your Home—Jonathan Erickson

"...an idea book, filled with sensible advice on what makes a home valuable."—San Francisco Examiner

The author profiles the three basic types of home buyers, defines the factors that affect resale value, explains two basic methods of determining your home's resale value, and shows you what rooms play the biggest role in deciding the value of a home. 208 pages, 105 illustrations. Book No. 3073, $14.95 paperback, $23.95 hardcover

KITCHEN REMODELING—A Do-It-Yourselfer's Guide—Paul Bianchina

"...offers all the know-how you need to remodel a kitchen economically and attractively."—Country Accents

Create a kitchen that meets the demands of your lifestyle. With this guide you can attractively and economically remodel your kitchen yourself. All the know-how you need is supplied in this complete step-by-step reference, from planning and measuring to installation and finishing. 206 pages, 187 illustrations. Book No. 3011, $14.95 paperback, $23.95 hardcover

FENCES, DECKS AND OTHER BACKYARD PROJECTS—2nd Edition—Dan Ramsey

Do-it-yourself—design, build, and landscape fences and other outdoor structures. The most complete guide available for choosing, installing, and properly maintaining every kind of fence imaginable. Plus, there are how-tos for a variety of outdoor structures, from sheds and decks to greenhouses and gazebos. Easy-to-follow instructions, work-in progress diagrams, tables, and hundreds of illustrations. 304 pages, Illustrated. Book No. 2778, $14.95 paperback, $22.95 hardcover

ATTIC, BASEMENT AND GARAGE CONVERSION: A Do-It-Yourselfer's Guide—Paul Bianchina

Achieve the space, appearance, and functional practicality you want in your home using the space that already exists in your home. This book combined with your own creative imagination will produce professional results. Information on tools and techniques is featured along with complete step-by-step instructions for converting underutilized basements, garages, and attics into spacious, attractive living spaces. 208 pages, Illustrated, with 8-color photo section. Book No. 3271, $16.95 paperback, $24.95 hardcover

WHAT'S IT WORTH: A Home Inspection and Appraisal Manual—Joseph V. Scaduto

"...replete with diagrams and written in language that can be understood by even the most novice house seeker...a must for anyone looking at older houses."—The Boston Globe

"...a truly no-nonsense manual for home buyers to use in a self-inspection process."—New York Public Library, New Technical Books

This book is packed with practical advice that could save you hundreds, even thousands of dollars in unexpected home maintenance and repair costs! 288 pages, 299 illustrations. Book No. 3301, $16.95 paperback, $24.95 hardcover

BASIC BLUEPRINTING READING—John A. Nelson

With the knowledge gained from this book, you will become expert at reading not only mechanical drawings, but construction, electrical, and plumbing drawings as well. Using a step-by-step approach, John Nelson incorporates the latest ANSI drafting standards as he covers all aspects of blueprint reading. Through straightforward language and excellent example illustrations, Nelson shows you how to identify and understand one-view, multi-view, sectional-view, and auxiliary-view drawings. 256 pages, 235 illustrations. Book No. 3273, $18.95 paperback, $27.95 hardcover

GARAGES: Complete Step-by-Step Building Plans—Ernie Bryant

A tremendous savings if you elect to contract out the project are the five building plans included in this book for garages in cape, colonial, and contemporary styles. One-, two-, and three-car garages, with or without living quarters above, are featured. These plans used with Bryant's explicit, illustrated, step-by-step instructions make it possible for you to build an attractive garage without the added cost of hiring professional help. 192 paperback, 127 illustrations. Book No. 3314, $14.95 paperback, $22.95 hardcover

MAKE YOUR HOUSE RADON FREE—Drs. Carl and Barbara Giles

Safeguard your home and family from the dangers of radon using this practical guide. What radon is, what it does, how it enters your home or workplace, how to remove it, and how to prevent it from recurring are covered in detail. Specific brands of radon-measuring and radon-deterring equipment, products, and materials are recommended. Tips on building a radon resistant home are also included. 144 pages, Illustrated. Book No. 3291, $9.95 paperback, $15.95 hardcover

KITCHEN AND BATHROOM CABINETS
—Percy W. Blandford

Kitchen and Bathroom Cabinets is a collection of wooden cabinet projects that will help your organize and modemize your kitchen and bathroom and make them more attractive at the same time. Clear step-by-step instructions and detailed drawings enable you to build wall and floor cabinets and counters, corner cupboards, island units, built-in tables, worktables, breakfast bars, vanities, and more. 300 pages, 195 illustrations. Book No. 3244, $16.95 paperback, $26.95 hardcover

PROFESSIONAL PLUMBING TECHNIQUES
—**Illustrated and Simplified**— Arthur J. Smith
"...useful for the experienced handyperson or the homeowner who wishes to verify an estimate of work needed."—**Booklist**

This plumbers companion includes literally everything from changing a washer to installing new fixtures: installing water heaters, water softners, dishwashers, gas stoves, gas dryers, grease traps, clean outs, and more. Includes helpful piping diagrams, tables and charts. 294 pages, 222 illustrations. Book No. 1763, $11.95 paperback, $16.95 hardcover

Look for These and Other TAB Books at Your Local Bookstore

To Order Call Toll Free 1-800-822-8158

(in PA and AK call 717-794-2191)

or write to TAB BOOKS Inc., Blue Ridge Summit, PA 17294-0840.